Creating Careers with Confidence

EDWARD ANTHONY COLOZZI

PEARSON

Prentice Hall

UPPER SADDLE RIVER, NEW JERSEY
COLUMBUS, OHIO

Library of Congress Cataloging-in-Publication Data

Colozzi, Edward Anthony.
  Creating careers with confidence / Edward Anthony Colozzi.
    p. cm.
  Includes bibliographical references.
  ISBN-13: 978-0-13-515789-3 (pbk.)
  ISBN-10: 0-13-515789-7 (pbk.)
  1. Vocational education—United States. 2. School-to-work transition—
United States. I. Title.
  LC1045.C626 2009
  370.1130973—dc22

                                                      2008022392

Vice President and Executive Publisher: Jeffery W. Johnston
Executive Editor: Sande Johnson
Editorial Assistant: Lynda Cramer
Senior Managing Editor: Pamela D. Bennett
Project Manager: Kerry J. Rubadue
Production Coordinator: Thistle Hill Publishing Services, LLC
Design Coordinator: Diane C. Lorenzo
Cover Design: Diane Lorenzo
Cover Image: Jeff Vanik
Operations Specialist: Susan W. Hannahs
Director of Marketing: Quinn Perkson
Senior Marketing Manager: Amy Judd
Marketing Coordinator: Brian Mounts

This book was set in Sabon by Aptara®, Inc. It was printed and bound by Bind-Rite Graphics/Robbinsville.
The cover was printed by Phoenix Color Corp./Hagerstown.

Photo Credits: Dave King © Dorling Kindersley, p. xv; Alistair Duncan © Dorling Kindersley, p. 7;
© Dorling Kindersley, p. 82.

Pearson® is a registered trademark of Pearson plc
Merrill® is a registered trademark of Pearson Education, Inc.

Pearson Education Ltd., London   Pearson Education North Asia, Ltd., Hong Kong
Pearson Education Singapore, Pte. Ltd.   Pearson Education de Mexico, S.A. de C.V.
Pearson Education Canada, Inc.   Pearson Education Malaysia, Pte. Ltd.
Pearson Education—Japan   Pearson Education Upper Saddle River, New Jersey
Pearson Education Australia PTY Limited

10 9 8 7 6 5 4 3 2 1
ISBN-13: 978-0-13-515789-3
ISBN-10:   0-13-515789-7

Dedication
To all the students and clients with whom
I've worked—from whom I learn so much

A PERSONAL LETTER TO YOU FROM ME

I want to share a few thoughts as you are about to take this important step in your own self-guided career exploration and planning. This is a personal journey through your crossroads of career-life choices and there are no right or wrong answers. I have written this workbook with the intention of being your companion and guide. The main angel character introduced in "The Choice" represents your companion. As she discovers and learns about herself, so will you. At the end of this workbook, *both* she and you will discover something about each other!

SELF-ASSESSMENT AND REFLECTION

I also want to discuss *self-assessed* skills or abilities. You might be wondering, "How valuable are my self-assessed abilities? Maybe I'm not the best judge, and perhaps I should take some sort of abilities test. I can give an opinion about my interests, what I enjoy, and my values, what's important to me—but how accurate are my self-estimates of my abilities?" These are normal questions. The following list presents a few things to consider in response to those questions. This information is fully discussed in the *Career Planning Survey Technical Manual* (American College Testing, 2001).

1. Ability test batteries typically assess only three to six abilities beyond the three R's (reading, writing, and arithmetic or math) and have limited usefulness in comprehensive, work-world searches for compatible person–environment matches. Research indicates there are many work-relevant abilities beyond those typically assessed by tests.

2. Many experts agree with Donald Super's assertion more than 40 years ago that in choosing an occupation, one is, in effect, choosing a means of implementing a self-concept and *not* choosing a means of implementing one's test scores! More about Super's ideas later.

3. Ability self-estimates can make work-relevant self-concepts evident to the person making the self-estimates (the client) and her or his counselor—and their validity can *exceed* that of test scores.

4. Test scores are usually based on operationally narrow exercises—for example, clerical perception tests use such words as *rapid digit-string* or *name matching*. In contrast, self-estimates are more broadly defined in work-relevant terms, similar to the broad definitions described in this workbook. (See, for instance, the self-assessment Banyan Branches activities in Part I.)

5. There is a consistent trend among leading assessment theorists to encourage greater use of self-assessment data. Research indicates that this will contribute significantly to the field of psychological assessment.

Your self-assessment is a valid and meaningful component in the career-life exploration and planning activities that you will be experiencing throughout this workbook. The more you take time to reflect on the various workbook activities, the more insight you will gain into yourself, your personality type, and how best to discover the most appropriate career-life matches.

NORMALCY

Finally, as I reflect over my many years of counseling young and older adults in transition, the most common statements I hear from people experiencing angst about their career-life situations are "I want a new direction"; "I'm at a crossroads"; "I want more purpose and meaning from my work"; "I seek more balance in my life"; or "I want more fulfillment from my work." You probably have similar feelings and thoughts. Be at peace. Be hopeful. You are very normal and have some very common feelings.

I have devoted my life to dealing with people's innate need to discover their callings and to be paid adequately for contributing their gifts in ways that provide meaning and purpose, to achieve more balance across life roles, and to learn how to believe in themselves again. The process you will undergo throughout this workbook will help you change your life.

I join with you and collaborate with you through my words, your reflections, your life story and themes, and your desire to change the course of your life journey. Use this workbook with a passion for living, and be challenged by it. Enjoy it and let it lead you to places where you know you belong. Treat this as your own mini-course on *you*—a guide to help you get your life on track and be successful. Good luck and happy career-life exploration and planning!

– EAC

For additional information and support, contact the author at 877-6-WISHES or www.lifeworkps.com/edwardc

CONTENTS

TABLE OF EXERCISES

Use this Table of Exercises as a guide to review your workbook progress. Check each box after you have completed the corresponding exercise. Your instructor/counselor might want to write a note to you in your workbook as it is reviewed from time to time.

ABOUT THE AUTHOR

Ed Colozzi is a career-life counselor whose special interests are career development—helping people discover their callings, meaning, and purpose across career and life roles—and the creation of multimedia guidance materials for use in education, agency, and business settings as well as the home environment.

He has taught career development courses at the undergraduate and graduate levels and has provided in-service training and consultation to a wide variety of professionals in K–12, college, agency, and corporate settings. His 30 years of counseling and teaching include experience at Barnard College, Columbia University, Borough of Manhattan Community College at CUNY, the University of Hawaii, Chaminade University, Bunker Hill Community College, and Leeward Community College, where he served as the coordinator of the Career Development Center for 10 years.

Ed served on the Governor's Manpower Commission on Full Employment, State of Hawaii, for seven years and was project director for the pilot site of Career Kokua, a computerized career information system used extensively throughout Hawaii. He also served as project director for a mini–field test of Discover II, a national computer guidance system developed by JoAnn Harris-Bowlsbey and currently owned and distributed by the American College Testing (ACT) Program. He pioneered the career-life focus and the use of computerized career guidance throughout Hawaii and the Pacific Basin region in the late 1970s.

Born and raised in the Boston area, Ed earned his B.A. degree in Psychology from Boston University, a master's degree in Counseling Psychology with a specialty in Vocational Rehabilitation Counseling, and a second master's and his doctorate in Higher Education from Teachers College, Columbia University.

He is a nationally certified counselor (NCC), a licensed mental health counselor (MAMHC), a certified trainer for Massachusetts, a master career counselor (MCC), and a National Career Development Association (NCDA) Fellow.

Ed is the founder and owner of Career Development and Counseling Services, presently located in Winchester, Massachusetts. He also provides consultation services to national and multinational clients. He has created Internet-based career guidance materials and a career guidance game for middle school students, and has worked closely with several projects involving the development of statewide standards for career development. Moreover, Ed is a national trainer for several associations including the National Career Development Association and the American Counseling Association, and he offers motivational presentations to a variety of school, college, agency, and corporate settings.

Ed has authored numerous articles, book chapters, and most recently a monograph that is being published by the National Career Development Association (NCDA) on DOVE (Depth-Oriented Values Extraction), a values clarification process that he created in 1978 and has used extensively with thousands of students and clients over the years.

You may contact Ed directly, toll-free, at 1-877-6-WISHES to speak with him. Or you can e-mail him at careercoachcolozzi@verizon.net, or visit his Web site at http://lifeworkps.com/edwardc.

ACKNOWLEDGMENTS

A very special word of appreciation to Sande Johnson for her invaluable inspiration, belief, guidance, and willingness to work closely with me to bring this workbook to publication. Sande has been a very dear friend and a life mentor.

Also, especially to JoAnn Harris-Bowlsbey, Donald Super, Darrell Luzzo, Mark Savickas, Lee Richmond, Spencer Niles, David Blustein, Dale Prediger, Angela Byars-Winston, Gary Klein, Rich Feller, Ronelle Langley, Michael Regan, Darlene Martin, Gemma Williams, Sally Gelardin, Pate Hubbard, Phyllis Dayao, Sybil Kyi, Earl Nishiguchi, Deneen Pennington, and the NCDA Executive Staff, for their important personal inspiration to me and for their professional contribution to career development theory and practice.

To Ed Pei, Michael Murakoshi, Michael Gross, Camille Gouldberg, Julie Glowacki, Pat and Dale Cramer, Dolly and David Langen, and Bob and Carla Fishman, for their special encouragement, support, and friendship over the years, and to John Holland, Ken Hoyt, Don Creamer, Bruce McKinlay, Elwood Chapman, and Dick Bolles, for their life's work that has touched many lives.

To my colleagues at the University of Hawaii and Leeward Community College, for their assistance and cooperation when the first versions of this workbook were field-tested.

Also to the Student Services and Cooperative Education staff at the Borough of Manhattan Community College at CUNY, where much of my practical experience with people in transition really began; to Saint Sebastian's Country Day School, which prepared me so well for the undergraduate and graduate education I was to enjoy; and to the faculty at Teachers College, Columbia University, who exposed me to the theoretical dynamics involved in the vocational choice process.

A special note of gratitude to Boston University, a truly great university that fosters the very essence of career-life exploration, provides support for the undecided searching student, and demands excellence through the inspiration of its dedicated faculty and staff. My undergraduate years at Boston University taught me the meaning of "self" and helped me with my personal career-life directions.

I would also like to thank the reviewers: Jennifer Anton, Webster University; JoAnn Harris-Bowlsbey, Career Development Leadership Alliance; Walter Buboltz, Louisiana Tech University; Connie Egelman, Nassau Community College; Sue Ekberg, Career Focus Inc.; Carol Giergerich, College of DuPage; and Barbara Storm, Fullerton College.

I thank my parents and sisters and brothers, who have helped me learn and grow in my understanding of the career-life process, and my children Marc, Michael, and Kristen, my true inspirations for so much that I do in my life. I know God better through the gifts of my three children, my life mentors from early on. Finally to Melani Lyn, MMBBEGFE. You have made all the difference in all the most important ways in my life.

THE CHOICE

Whether you believe in God, angels, guides, the Buddha within, Atman, universal love and energy that unites all life, the beauty and life-force of nature, none of this, all of this, part of this—or if you have no idea at all and feel clueless—welcome to the Life Journey. The truth is that you are here right now on this planet. I believe you are here for a reason. You might agree or disagree, or you might be unsure. Read the following fable, "The Choice," and do not attach any judgment to the outcome. Just relax for a few minutes and allow your inner voice to respond to the story. Consider the idea that, like the characters in this story, you are on this planet for a reason—to fulfill some unique role or life mission. Note how self-awareness, self-confidence, and willingness to take on calculated risk enter into the decision-making process used by the main angel character in the fable.

–Edward Anthony Colozzi (EAC)

A long, long time ago, in a faraway galaxy known as Genesis, the Creator called a very special gathering of all the angels. This was a significant event because it was from this gathering that creation was to unfold.

Each angel would be allowed to choose whatever role she or he desired in the plan for creation. The possibilities included becoming planets, suns, stars, comets, and the like—and a comprehensive explanation of all the choices was presented so the angels could have enough information about the alternatives. After all, when you're deciding whether to be a brilliant sun or a fiery shooting star, that's serious business. You need to explore all the facts about your options before making your selection.

So each angel listened carefully and took notes as the various roles were discussed.

The first role described was that of the great burning suns. Each of these suns would provide light for an entire solar system and serve as its center. An enviable role indeed!

Another role would be a planet with the freedom to move about and orbit its sun. There were to be many, many planets throughout the different galaxies, differing in size and color and each having unique characteristics, except that none would be responsible for sustaining any life-forms. Many angels whispered their excitement at the prospect of becoming a planet.

A third role involved becoming a special planet—one that would have the responsibility of sustaining life, of governing the tides of its great oceans, of harnessing the winds and providing vegetation and sufficient cloud cover to protect the planet and all life-forms that were to develop there.

This planet would have intelligent life-forms to be called *human beings* who would thrive and multiply. There was a quiet hush as the last few details of this third unique role were explained, and then a low murmur of concern from 100 billion angels swept through the gathering like a slow, rolling thunderclap. This could hardly be the choice of any angel!

This serious concern soon vanished when the gathering heard the fourth role: to become a genuine star! This role would permit countless angels to light up the universe with their brilliance and fiery dazzle, each star larger than most of the giant suns of the solar systems, and capable of being seen from galaxies light-years away. This role appeared to be the popular choice of many angels.

A fifth role involved becoming special mini-stars to be called *comets*, which would race and dart about at light speeds throughout the galaxies to help light up the darkness of space and make the nights come alive with movement. These fiery objects would have spectacular dust tails more than 10 million miles long!

The angels were then informed that they did not have to choose any of those five roles. They could choose a sixth role: to remain angels and assist creation wherever and whenever appropriate. This seemed like a reasonable choice for many of the angels, because they were already happy to be playing the role they had originally been given.

After all six roles had been explained and the time for choosing was at hand, there was a great clamor. It was evident that some order would have to be brought about immediately if this plan for creation was really to unfold. Six separate groupings were designated to facilitate the division of preferences.

An abundance of angels jumped forth and chose to gather in the first group, where they were to become the great suns of the solar systems.

Many others gathered immediately in the group that was to become the variety of planets orbiting the suns.

The largest group of all, millions and millions, gathered together in anticipation of becoming the twinkling stars that would light up the heavens.

Many millions chose to be the fiery comets with dazzling tails that would sweep through the universe.

Of course, millions of other angels decided to remain angels and gathered in their appropriate group.

The excitement and level of dialogue began to decrease as everyone noticed that no one had selected the third role: the planet that was to sustain life.

When some time had passed and still no angel had chosen the third role, angels from each of the other groups began expressing their opinions about the situation.

"I'm very satisfied with my choice. Being a planet will allow me to express my uniqueness within a solar system of my choice," explained one angel.

"I'm delighted with the idea of becoming a star," said another, "because I feel it's important to share my brilliance with other stars and combine our capacities to light up the heavens."

Others expressed similar sentiments, including those who chose to remain as angels—each giving some very good reasons for her or his preference.

Then several angels began to reflect on the great responsibility associated with the third role, especially since life-forms would be involved. They spoke of the strong sense of commitment it would take to work with the many factors facing that unique planet.

They talked of the planning that would be required and the great amount of patience needed to withstand the test of time and human error as evolution on the planet occurred.

Some angels expressed concern that only an angel with a realistic self-concept and an understanding of her or his balance with the environment could possibly take on such a role.

The most common feeling expressed by the angels was a lack of readiness. Many said that's what prevented them from seriously considering the third role. They needed time to gain more self-confidence, self-knowledge, and perhaps even learn more about what it might mean to become a life-sustaining planet.

The Creator exclaimed aloud, "What a dilemma! Here we are at the moment of creation and we can't find one angel who wants to become this new planet. What are we going to do?"

Just then, a little angel edged herself out from those who had decided to remain angels. She slowly walked up to the Creator and declared, "I've been listening carefully to what's been shared here. We've been at this six days now, and I've put a lot of thought and reflection into my decision, and it feels right for me to do this.

"Even though I've been very satisfied with being an angel, I've decided that it's more important for me to take up some new challenges. I want to find some new outlets for my interests and what I want to be doing with my talents, energy, and time. I want something with even more meaning and purpose.

"I don't have all the answers now, but I'm willing to learn. I want to move myself in a new direction with this great creation you are planning for all of us. And what's more important, I really feel that I'm ready to choose this—if you'll give me a chance."

And in the twinkling of a star, creation had its beginning, because a little angel stepped forward and said, "I'm ready."

This fable is a metaphor for making career-life choices. There are thousands of jobs and multiple life roles you will be considering throughout your life span. You will need to assess information about yourself and your options as you make important decisions that will affect your future.

Everyone on the planet gets to do this, so you are not alone—but it sure feels like you're all alone when you experience some of the angst that arises as you deal with your decisions. The unknown can often trigger feelings of anxiety, fear, low self-confidence, and even helplessness. On the other hand, sometimes the unknown can trigger feelings of excitement and hopefulness about possibilities and new beginnings. Note your own responses to the unknown, because your feelings influence your attitude and behavior.

The main task at hand is to be successful with your exploration and planning efforts so you can enjoy clarity, focus, and new directions. This will increase your self-confidence and will greatly facilitate your academic success and your work success—and will also increase your chances for discovering a fulfilling life.

Just as described in the fable, all the possible jobs in the world can be assigned to six groups that also match six similar personality types. Most people are dominant in two or three of these six personality types and can easily discover the appropriate person–environment matches that will provide income and lead to fulfillment.

One factor is the most important and leads to successful career-life exploration and planning. This factor is *readiness*. Either you are ready to engage yourself in this process and take the necessary actions to move forward—even if it's using those important baby steps—or your are not ready.

You don't need all or even a few of the answers at this stage. You don't need all or even a little bit of the information at this stage. You don't need all or even a little bit of self-confidence at this stage. You might want all these things, but you don't need them.

You do need to feel in your heart that you are indeed ready to set out and explore, while remaining open to new possibilities. If you are reading this workbook now, you are most likely ready to move forward, and this workbook will facilitate your journey of discovery and success.

INTRODUCTION AND OVERVIEW

THE PURPOSE OF THIS WORKBOOK IS TO HELP YOU MORE EASILY DISCOVER YOUR PURPOSE AND YOUR CALLING.

INTRODUCTION TO ALL PERSONS USING THIS WORKBOOK

If you are a college student between the ages of 17 and 21 or a high school senior who is serious about career exploration, continue reading the discussion that follows under the heading "To Students." It will provide you with a useful framework for successfully completing the career exploration activities in your workbook.

If you are an older college student and consider yourself an adult in transition, read the discussion that follows under "To Students," as well as the discussion titled "To Adults in Transition."

To Students

Dear Student,

Your workbook is designed to help you accomplish effective career exploration and planning activities that will lead to success in the classroom and in planning your career. It addresses key topics that will benefit any student who chooses to explore her or his options regarding work or additional schooling.

One of the main decisions you face, whether graduating from high school or college, is deciding which direction to follow. You can imagine the possible options as being behind three separate doors: Door #1 (School-to-Work), Door #2 (School-to-School), and Door #3 (School-to-Other). Selecting one door over the others doesn't mean you cannot choose one of the other two doors later. Each choice has consequences, however. The consequences might be either positive or negative and will directly affect your future. The three basic alternatives are discussed below for your consideration.

Door #1: School-to-Work

Choosing the school-to-work door means seeking and obtaining employment directly after school. This will involve assessing your top skills, interests, and values—especially your work values—so you can decide what jobs and career paths best match your personality, your goals, and your plans for the future. Your work might be in an office, a hospital or health care facility, a museum, a classroom, an engineering firm, an auto repair shop, an art gallery, a gym or other recreational setting, a shopping mall, or perhaps the military. Most people today will have 7 to 10 jobs representing three or four different career fields by the time they retire in their seventies! With more than 22,000 different jobs from which to choose, selecting the "right" path can be confusing and stressful.

Part of the solution is to narrow down the options to a group of possibilities that seem to be a close match to your personality, your career and life goals, and your dreams. As you learn more about your own personality type, your likes and dislikes, your special talents, and other factors, making choices will be easier. You will have more confidence about your choices and about being in charge of your future and your life.

When you are ready to find a job, whatever it is and wherever the setting, you will need to let people know that you are seeking employment. Usually a cover letter, a résumé, and a job interview are the stepping-stones to a successful job search. The Internet can be useful because it provides numerous resources with useful links that will provide you with important job-seeking information.

Networking Learning how to network—to meet people in the field of work you are considering—is very helpful. One technique is called an informational networking interview and another is called a job-networking interview. The informational interview allows you to explore information about a potential job and career path, while also letting people know you might be looking for a job in that particular area. It is wise to do a few informational interviews before setting up any job-seeking interviews. Job interviews are appropriate when you are in the process of actively seeking employment.

Both of these techniques involve networking because you are meeting people who will have information useful for your career exploration. These people might have a job for you, or might know someone who has a job for you, or might know someone who knows someone else who has a job for you. When you meet all these people, you are joining a network that already existed—long before you met the first person you contacted. Joining their network will help you in your career exploration and job-seeking activities.

Fighting for Equal Pay Jobs translate into income, and it is important to be aware of something called the *wage gap* as you think about obtaining a job. The wage gap compares the earnings of women and people of various races and ethnicities to the earnings of white males, a group generally not subject to race-based or sex-based discrimination. The wage gap is expressed as a percentage—and the higher the percentage, the better (as it nears 100%, the wage gap is approaching zero). For instance, in 1963, women earned only 58% as much as men. This is unfair. One would hope the wage gap had disappeared or at least diminished over the ensuing 45+ years.

In 1963 the Equal Pay Act (EPA) was signed by President John F. Kennedy, making it illegal for employers not to pay the same wages to men and women who hold the same job and do the same work. As just stated in the preceding paragraph, at the time of the EPA's passage women earned only 58 cents for every dollar earned by men. Currently, that rate has increased to only 77%—an improvement of less than half a penny a year. The disparity is even greater for women of color.

Some estimates indicate that if women actually did earn the same as men who work the same number of hours, are the same age, have the same education and union status, and live in the same region of the country, their annual family incomes would rise by approximately $4,000. In turn, this would reduce poverty rates in America by half—a noble goal indeed. The wage gap is unfair and must change! Women and men alike must be informed and must be willing to fight for equal pay for equal work.

If you believe your best option after school is Door #1, this workbook will help you with these and related topics that support your successful school-to-work decisions.

Door #2: School-to-School

Choosing the school-to-school door involves seeking and obtaining more education and training directly after you complete high school or college. It also involves assessing your top skills, interests, and values—so you can decide what education and training path will best match your personality, your goals, and your plans for the future. With so many undergraduate or graduate majors and subjects from which to choose, selecting the "right" major can be confusing and stressful.

Part of the solution is to narrow down the options to a group of possibilities that seem to be a close match to your personality type, your career and life goals, and your dreams. It is common and acceptable practice to come to college undecided about a major area of study. After all, one of the purposes of college is to explore your possible career and life goals. *Leaving* college totally undecided, on the other hand, is not acceptable. Figuring out your direction requires intentional career exploration on your part.

Choosing the best undergraduate or graduate major or program will enable you to surround yourself with topics, discussions, and like-minded people. You will typically find this to be quite motivational. You will likely be more willing to devote the required time to your studies to reap the rewards of good grades for your efforts. This level of engagement will likely push you to persist to graduation even if the road becomes rough.

Working While Going to School It is expensive to attend college, and the time and energy you spend attending college is time you cannot spend earning income. Unless you are independently wealthy, you will need some source of income to sustain your lifestyle. Although a college education has many benefits—including increased lifetime earnings and increased opportunities for a variety of employment possibilities—attending college usually means that you cannot accept full-time employment. On the other hand, furthering your education is an excellent investment of time and energy. The key is to make the best use of your time while attending college.

Some schools encourage students to participate in an employment setting while they are enrolled in their degree program. One such program—*cooperative education* (or *co-op*)—gives students a variety of options, including working part-time while taking classes or working full-time one semester and then attending school one semester, alternating work with full-time enrollment in classes. In addition, many colleges offer internships for a semester. These are excellent ways to experience the world of work and to network with employers who might provide a job offer after graduation based on your internship experience.

Getting the Most from Your Education Whether you are enrolled in undergraduate or graduate studies, the responsibility for achieving success falls squarely on *you*. You need to make your needs known, to seek help when you need it, to put in the necessary hours of studying for your courses so you are successful, and to discipline your time and take charge of your college experience and your life. Once you have successfully obtained your education and training, you will most likely want to follow the general plan outlined in Door #1 and implement your school-to-work decision. Education is lifelong, however. You should always be open to acquiring whatever education and training is needed to remain competitive in the job market.

If you believe your best option after school is Door #2, this workbook will help you with the topics that support your successful school-to-school decisions—including dealing with stress, time management, and developing an academic advising plan that helps you choose the appropriate courses to match your career goals.

Door #3: School-to-Other

Choosing the school-to-other door involves reviewing and selecting the best options immediately after school that do *not* involve paid employment or further education or training. These choices might include marriage, travel, volunteer work, or perhaps something else. This decision will still require assessing your top skills, interests, and values—so you can decide on a path that best matches your personality, your goals, and your plans for the future. When you are ready to obtain a job or continue with your education or training, you will most likely want to follow the general plans outlined in Doors #1 and #2.

If you believe you best option after school is Door #3, this workbook will help you with these and related topics that support your successful school-to-other decisions. It will also prepare you for dealing with Doors #1 and #2 at a later date.

To Adults in Transition

Dear Adult in Transition,

Your workbook is designed to help you accomplish effective career exploration and planning activities that will lead to success in dealing with your career and life transitions. Every transition begins with an "ending"—and this usually includes ending old rules or ways of thinking, behaving, and experiencing life.

Most people desire rules. When they experience the endings of old rules, they immediately seek new rules. Transitions take time, however, and there can be a lag period between the endings of old rules and the formation of new ones. When people experience an absence of rules, they often feel uncomfortable. During a time of transition it is useful to recognize this feeling of discomfort and reflect on where you have been, where you presently are, and where you want to go as you move forward with your life journey.

Most people's transitions involve job changes but can also involve relationship changes. In addition, transitions might involve a change in residence. They might involve health-related concerns such as becoming a caregiver to a loved one. All these transitions present both a challenge and an opportunity—to be patient and yet be sufficiently disciplined to take charge and take the steps that are needed to successfully navigate the new challenges.

Having clarity about your current skills, interests, and values—especially your work values—will guide your decisions. The numerous jobs and fields from which to choose, along with the extenuating circumstances that are often interwoven into the fabric of making the "right" choices, can be confusing and stressful. Part of the solution is to narrow down the options to a group of possibilities that seem to be a close match to your personality, your career and life goals, and your dreams for a more fulfilling and balanced life. As you learn more about your own personality type, your likes and dislikes, your special talents, and other factors, making choices will be easier. You will have more confidence about your choices and about being in charge of your future and your life.

This shift often requires retooling and reschooling. Many adults are taking advantage of higher education as a stepping-stone to more lucrative and fulfilling careers following transitions that might involve divorce, relocation, or simply the desire to pursue unfulfilled career-related dreams after successfully raising their families.

Your workbook will help you with these and related topics that support your successful transition—including dealing with stress, time management, and obtaining balance among your many career-life roles.

What's at Stake for You?

Career-life exploration and planning—that sounds like something to do with the unknown. True! Most of us feel like we're at a crossroads more than a few times throughout our life journey, and we aren't quite sure where to turn. But this process can mean discovery, awareness, confirmation of present directions, and even new directions and getting your life on track, especially regarding education and work. What's at stake is your future, your happiness, and your success. Congratulations on choosing to be more proactive in creating the life path that can maximize your potential! Let's begin!

A USEFUL AND IMPORTANT SHIFT IN THINKING ABOUT CAREERS

The old way of defining a career was, "What I do from 9 to 5, pays me bucks, and hopefully I'll like it." This notion no longer works. Today, informed individuals know they have choices and will make these choices across multiple career and life roles in ways that lead to success. People desperately want a career with some purpose. They want the opportunity to contribute their gifts to others directly or indirectly, while enjoying an appropriate income source and a balanced life. It is definitely possible to create a life with this balance in mind.

The term *career-life* refers to all the roles you might be playing right now in your life, including time spent as a student, part-time or full-time worker, homemaker, spouse, parent, or any of a variety of other roles. More about this later.

Most of us make many important career-life decisions throughout our lives. Making career-life choices means being ready to honestly look at who you are and where you want to go with your life.

It means deciding that you want to do something about your future.

It means taking time to sort out some important questions and discover answers to those questions.

It means hard work and effort over time, often involving sacrifices.

But it also means experiencing personal growth and satisfaction, and feeling better about yourself and the fact that you have gained more control over your life's direction.

It means learning to believe in yourself!

It means redefining what success means to you in the context of earning an income in a fulfilling work role, while experiencing balance among all your career-life roles.

A PROVEN AND TESTED CAREER-LIFE STRATEGY

To make wise and informed career-life choices, you need a theory-based, integrated, and practical strategy. The key components covered in this workbook are based on sound research and the very best of career development theory. Thousands of persons have successfully used the concepts presented in *Creating Careers with Confidence* in numerous settings. Here you will find time-tested career exploration activities that are aimed at people dealing with multiple career changes in a new economy—people who desire meaningful work, appropriate income, a sense of balance across life roles, and more fulfillment. The five main components of the Career-Life Strategy are as follows:

■ **Self-knowledge:** Discovering information about yourself, your skills, your interests and values—your personality type. This involves discovering your own life story, who you are, and what you are called to do in this life. Your life story involves themes.

- **The world-of-work:** Learning important information about the world-of-work, including how it is organized and the various occupations that comprise it. Your themes will match the world-of-work.

- **Career-life concept:** Understanding the career-life concept and the different roles that make up your career, including the work role. This component allows you to integrate your life experiences with balance, providing an outlet for the flow of your life-force energy. This results in feeling purposeful and produces fulfillment, less stress, and a higher-functioning immune system. You will be healthier and happier.

- **Person–environment match:** Discovering and/or creating the best person–environment matches for yourself across all career-life roles. One way to locate the right career path is to narrow down and discover the best matches from among those that most closely match you and your personality type. Another way is to create what you need and want—creating your career—a powerful concept indeed! You can create a career from your life themes.

- **Decision-making processes:** Learning and using reflective and intuitive decision-making processes that are applicable to the other components and easy to apply throughout your life.

These five components are each represented by a symbol:

△ = a self-knowledge pyramid representing your self-assessed skills, interests, and values—in general, who you think you are and what you have to offer to the world. This self-knowledge △ is the key to achieving self-actualization and happiness throughout your life. It is important to gain an understanding of your self-knowledge △. Developing a sense of self takes effort, time, and sometimes assistance from others who are trained to help you. Culture, heredity, the environment, religious tradition, and other factors influence who you are, how you develop, and how you look at yourself. This includes the beliefs you have and choose to hold onto as well as the new beliefs you are willing to accept to lead you forward throughout your life journey. A sense of purpose lies deep within your self-knowledge △ and is waiting to be discovered.

⊕ = a pie-shaped figure representing the world-of-work and the way many occupations can be organized into very logical sections or pieces of the pie, sometimes referred to as *regions* of the world-of-work.

🌈 = a series of rainbow bands, each representing the different roles you play in life that make up your "career." These roles include, for example, the time and energy you put in as a part-time worker, as a student, and perhaps as a friend, spouse, and parent. You might actually be playing several of these roles at the same time, hence the term *career-life*. This component is easy to understand and also very enjoyable to apply to your personal career-life situation.

⟳ = a circular, clockwise arrow that represents the steps involved in a reflective and intuitive process of making decisions—especially those decisions that have serious consequences for you or others close to you. This component is easy to understand, easy to apply, and very effective—if you take the time to learn the process. The I, or "inner eye" in the center of this symbol, represents intuition. More discussion about intuition is presented in Part II.

◔ = a pie-shaped figure representing the way your self-knowledge △ matches with specific occupational environments in the world-of-work. These are called *person–environment matches.* You can look for these matches as you experience your work role or you can create appropriate matches for yourself—hence the title of this workbook: *Creating Careers with Confidence.*

When you place these five components together, you arrive at a very easy-to-understand formula:

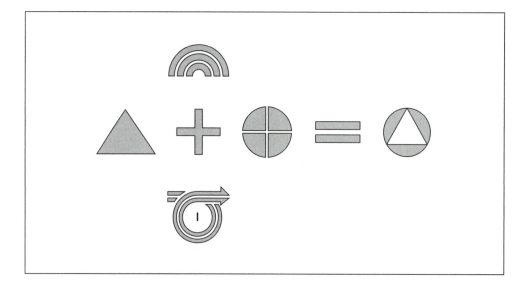

Briefly summarized, you first develop a sense of self and find out who you think you really are and what gives you a sense of purpose. Then you gain some understanding about the concept of career-life, how the world-of-work is organized, and how to make reflective and intuitive decisions. This new understanding will lead you to where you fit into the world-of-work.

Your task is to know yourself better, especially your skills, interests, and values—your personality type. Review the many career-life roles, including the work role you will be playing throughout most of your life. Understand the world-of-work and how occupations can be easily separated and divided into appropriate regions.

By putting all these components together, you end up with specific occupational clusters (groupings of similar occupations). Then you can more easily narrow down those occupational environments to those that match the type of person you are. These certain person–environment matches will nourish you and help make you a happier, more satisfied and productive person. Make sure to use a reflective and intuitive decision-making process, to make wise and informed choices. Doing this will increase the probability of achieving desired outcomes throughout your life.

Your options are either (1) to hope that time and chance will slowly fit you into a nourishing environment, or (2) to put in the effort yourself now to look for those nourishing environments.

The key is to achieve a balance in the simultaneous roles you play throughout your life and to allow for these roles, including your work role, to be an expression of who you are—your self-knowledge △. A rainbow is most beautiful to observe when the variety and richness of its colors are evident. Your life is most satisfactory and fulfilling when you balance it with a variety of roles that allow you to express who you are. This way, the time and energy you put into your career-life roles become an expression of yourself as you actually release yourself and your energy into each role. This physiological flow of energy is what brings fulfillment to your life and color to your career-life rainbow.

In order to balance your life and choose the roles to play—including choosing the "right" college major, the "right" occupation, or the "right" second or third career—you need to learn how to make wise and informed decisions about a variety of issues. And the bottom line in making those decisions is knowing what's most important to you. In other words, you must know your value system, the most important part of your self-knowledge ⊕.

Your value system clearly has the most powerful influence on all the career-life choices you have made in the past, are now making, and will continue to make throughout your life. Having a sense of purpose evolves from discernment of your values.

> *"What is success? I think it is a mixture of having flair for the thing that you are doing; knowing that it is not enough, that you have got to have hard work and a certain sense of purpose."*
>
> –MARGARET THATCHER

DISCOVERING YOUR LIFE STORY

This workbook has been carefully designed to help you rediscover things about yourself and your personal, unique life story. Everyone has a life story with several life themes.

Your life story begins with simply being born and initially being raised within a small group of people—your family. As time goes on, you experience different things, and themes or patterns begin to emerge. You work in groups, whether in an educational or a workplace environment. Your life story also includes everything that happens as you move from the initial small group that raised you to the much larger group of diverse people with whom you interact during your lifetime. Your life story underscores your personal journey. In a sense, the story provides the details that shape and direct your life's journey. The journey, therefore, becomes the continuous evolution of *you* as a unique human being with talents, interests, skills, and abilities. Your journey is the process that further defines and clarifies your life story—it is the amalgamation of you and all the steps you have taken along the way.

Recognizing your life story and its specific life-shaping themes requires reflection. This workbook is designed to help you properly reflect and learn about yourself, your story, and your life themes. You will learn how to develop a personal and practical plan that you can use again and again throughout your life for many career-life choices. You will learn more about yourself (skills, interests, and values) through various enjoyable exercises. You will begin to discover your personality type, referred to in this workbook as your *self-knowledge code*. You will also learn how the world-of-work is organized and how to identify the specific occupations that most closely match your self-knowledge code.

You will have an opportunity to better understand and assess the various career-life roles you are currently playing and discover effective ways to achieve more balance in your life. You will examine how a reflective decision-making process and your intuition can help you succeed in identifying and accomplishing present and future goals.

SPECIAL FEATURES OF THIS WORKBOOK

This workbook contains an easy and helpful strategy for informational interviews, including a few primer questions if you intend to seek contact with employers or otherwise enter the labor force. This section will be especially useful if you are interested in job shadowing (spending a workday as a "shadow," observing someone's job tasks) or cooperative education experiences that encourage visiting local work sites. More information about these programs can be obtained from your counselor or career center staff.

Part V of this workbook presents specific questions related to the occupations most closely suited to you. You will be able to fill in appropriate responses to each of the questions using the resources suggested in this workbook. Some of these resources are also available at your career center or library.

Part VII helps you list several realistic objectives related to your tentative occupational selection and encourages you to specify "Your Best Next Step," the one step that will activate your plan and get your life moving in the right direction.

The three appendixes provide important tools to help you move forward with career exploration and your subsequent action-planning involving academic advising and job-hunting activities:

■ *Appendix 1* allows you to track insights as you complete activities in this workbook. This will evolve into your personal career-life diary that will reveal important life themes.

■ *Appendix 2* allows you to create your *Ideal Career Scenario* based on the exercises completed throughout the workbook.

■ *Appendix 3* is designed as a personal portfolio to use in your education and work roles. It includes a résumé builder, an academic advising guide, and a personal coaching tool for time and stress management.

USEFUL RESOURCES TO HELP YOU COMPLETE YOUR WORKBOOK

This workbook is self-paced. You go at your own speed, depending on what's happening with the rest of your life. It can be used along with a career planning course you are now taking, or you can use it as a personal guidebook as you set out on your own to discover your calling, the education you need to prepare for your life's work, and the steps you must take to pull it all together.

Each part opener provides a convenient *Spotlight Summary* that highlights the key objectives to be covered. You should first complete the exercises in the workbook to narrow down your options before visiting the Internet sites or accessing the specific resources at your college to obtain occupational and labor market information. Reflecting on your personality type and matching world-of-work options will help to narrow down the choices to a few that can be easily and thoroughly researched using the suggested resources in the workbook.

There are many excellent written and audiovisual materials in your career center or library to help you plan a career. You might find a computer-assisted career guidance system (CACGS) such as DISCOVER or SIGI to be very helpful. Some of these programs—such as Career Kokua in Hawaii and Eureka in California—are modeled after the Oregon Career Information System. Others are known as G.I.S., COIN, or CHOICES. Your counselor can inform you about the availability of these materials at your college.

These computerized systems provide accurate and current career information about specific local and/or national labor markets—including descriptions of occupational duties, important aptitudes, work settings, hiring practices, current employment, wages, and job outlook or demand data. Preparation and training information such as special licensing, required skills, and related educational programs are also often included. These systems are generally easy to use, and several sections of this workbook have been designed to work with most CACGSs.

The Internet sites suggested throughout this workbook provide excellent additional resources. One example is the Web site of the American College Testing Program, which provides important and useful links to the interactive *World-of-Work Map* used in this workbook.

One of the most powerful resources will be *your own ability and willingness* to reflect on the various workbook activities that have been carefully woven together to give you the opportunity to *tell* your life story, *hear* your own story, *notice* the themes, and *create* your careers with confidence.

YOUR RESULTS

Upon completion of this workbook, you should expect the following results:

- You will develop an awareness of a new and powerful career-life strategy that you can apply to your present and future directions—a strategy that emphasizes a new way of looking at the term *career*.

- You will discover deeper insights into your life story, your life themes, and your power of personal reflection to clarify your vision and raise your confidence— sometimes called *efficacy beliefs*.

- You will have a clearer understanding of self-knowledge, including your personality type and your self-assessed skills, interests, and values. This workbook uses a pyramid icon (△) to represent self-knowledge.

- You will have increased knowledge of the world-of-work and how it is organized, including relevant local and national labor market information. This knowledge will enable you to identify specific occupations that best suit you.

- You will learn about reflective and intuitive decision-making processes that you can reuse throughout your life. These processes emphasize the importance of planning ahead and the relationship between present and future events.

- You will begin to develop a personal network of employer contacts tailored to your career interests and goals.

- You will begin to develop a detailed action plan for implementing your career-life decisions, including *Your Best Next Step* for initiating your action plan, your academic course selection, and other important steps that move you in the right direction.

You will notice two icons inserted in various sections throughout the workbook. One of these icons (R) prompts you to individually reflect, and the other (R&S) prompts you to individually reflect and then share your reflections with others as directed by your instructor or counselor. Reflection is the most important activity you will do to achieve clarity and direction. Sharing your reflections and hearing others share their reflections helps to crystallize your own feelings and ideas.

YOUR BEGINNING . . . *REFLECTIONS*

All humans experience a life journey. No one's life journey is better or worse than another's. Each person's journey is unique. Some people might perceive their personal journey as better or worse than ours, but because they cannot have our unique experience, they cannot fully know how we experience our journey. We might share our experience, and at least we might try to seek some degree of empathy from others. But it is still our unique journey, our experience, and our decision about how we choose to experience it.

Every life journey has a *night journey*—a challenging time of darkness, perhaps loneliness, and some feelings of despair. The night journey is especially useful for growth and wisdom. At night we tend to move more slowly, drive more slowly, walk more carefully, listen more attentively, and open our eyes more widely. Our night journey is an important and fruitful time to reflect and will reap many rewards for us.

All humans reflect. Other life-forms seem to reflect as well. Observe any dog or cat waiting patiently to cross the street. Notice those amazing birds—pausing until the last possible moment, diving in front of your moving car just seconds before you pass them, and then managing to navigate themselves safely to the other side of the street without losing even one feather! Little squirrels, on the other hand, don't seem to exercise the art of reflection, as they attempt to cross the street facing oncoming traffic. Their memories must be very short.

Our memories are more perfect. It's our attempt to have immediate recall of all those memories that is imperfect. Reflection helps our efforts to discover important source memories. We need to slow down and listen to our heart, our mind, and mostly our spirit. *Reflecting* means listening to our inner voice, our true self, and taking time to notice what we are telling ourselves. Our reflections become the stepping-stones for our journey forward. They faithfully serve us during our waking and sleeping hours. Our reflections are our gifts.

They are even present when we choose not to pay attention to them. Life's distractions, especially difficult situations and relationships, can cover up our reflections, just as waves splashing over beach sand leave a perfectly polished, smooth, wet surface— for a few seconds. Then tiny air bubbles, little sand crabs, and other creatures immediately become visible, popping up everywhere until the next wave splashes over them and pushes them into a temporary state of apparent nonexistence. But those air bubbles and little sand crabs, just like our reflections, will be back to remind us "We're here! We are all part of life and your beach-walking experience today. You usually neglect to notice us—but if you pay closer attention to us, you will get much more out of your walk."

YOUR REFLECTIONS

Take at least 60 seconds—or better yet, three to five minutes—and close your eyes and ears to the outside world. Imagine yourself to be in a safe and comfortable environment, one you would thoroughly enjoy.

You might choose a peaceful spot on a hillside overlooking grassy fields, or on the sloping edge of a warm sand dune by the ocean, or on a dock dangling your feet into the cool water of a quiet lake, or near a snow-capped mountain where the trees are blanketed with fresh snow and the sunlight makes everything glisten and sparkle like billions of tiny diamonds. Go there now and feel that experience for a minute or more. Breathe in deeply through your nose, filling your diaphragm, and then exhale slowly, through your lips. Do this four or five times so you change your brain chemistry and body physiology. Become at peace.

Reflect on yourself and your present situation—where you are right now in your life journey. Are you at a crossroad, about to face some new and perhaps challenging experiences? How is it for you to be experiencing a career-life transition? What are your specific feelings—not thoughts, but *feelings* like sadness, frustration, joy, anger, excitement, confusion, desperation, or freedom?

Take a few minutes to reflect on your feelings. You might have many feelings, including some you consider positive and others negative. Continue on, and follow the instructions in the exercises that follow.

MY REFLECTIONS

On the lines provided below, write your reflections about your true feelings concerning where you are right now in your life journey. Do you have feelings such as excitement, hope, anxiety, or sadness? For example, if your true feelings include sadness, anger, or disappointment, what are your reflections about those feelings? Be honest, vulnerable, loving to yourself, and accepting that these feelings are part of who you are and your experiences at the present. Remember that feelings—like clouds that block the sunlight—move, break apart, and eventually disappear. They can return, but they always move on. Slow, deep breathing helps relieve strong negative feelings. Learning *not* to have attachment to your negative feelings is important to your physical, emotional, and spiritual states of well-being. Train yourself *not* to be tied down by the attachments that can snarl your life and block your free flow of energy from within. This is lifelong training, so just take baby steps each day. You will notice your progress and even experience giant steps now and then.

_____

_____

_____

_____

_____

MY MAIN SUMMARY REFLECTION IN ONE SENTENCE

Review your reflections above. Ask yourself, "What is the *main* message I am getting from myself as I review those statements?" Feel the inner wisdom that spoke to you when you wrote those reflections. Now, in the space provided below, using one sentence, write your *main summary* of the several reflections you just completed.

_____

_____

MY MAIN SUMMARY REFLECTION IN ONE TO THREE WORDS

Review the one-sentence main summary reflection you just wrote. Again, feel the inner wisdom that spoke to you when you wrote it. Ask yourself, "What is the *main* message I am getting from myself now as I review that main summary reflection? How can I express the truth and essence of that sentence in one to three words?"

Write those one to three words on the line provided below. Circle your response. Close your eyes, and say these words four or five times slowly as you breathe deeply, inhaling through your nose to expand your diaphragm and exhaling through your lips.

Now turn to Appendix 1 on page 91 and write your one to three words in the space provided under *My Main Summary Reflection in One to Three Words,* and then continue with this workbook.

POP QUIZ!

Take this pop quiz to check your knowledge about work, education, and job opportunities. The correct answers are given throughout this workbook, and you can fill them in as you discover them, and then compare them to your original answers.

YOUR QUESTION	YOUR GUESS	CORRECT ANSWER (to be filled in later)
How many different specific jobs are there in the world-of-work?	_____	_____
How many different jobs do most people have before they retire?	_____	_____
How many different career fields (education, sales, etc.) do most people experience in their work history?	_____	_____
How many jobs has the average 27-year-old experienced today?	_____	_____
What was the wage gap percentage (women's earnings relative to men's) in 1963 when the Equal Pay Act was signed by President John F. Kennedy?	_____	_____
What is the approximate wage gap today?	_____	_____
What *should be* the wage gap percentage?	_____	_____

PART

I

SELF-KNOWLEDGE:
LEARNING MORE ABOUT YOURSELF

IT'S IMPORTANT TO LEARN WHAT'S MOST IMPORTANT TO YOU!

"A PRUDENT QUESTION IS ONE-HALF OF WISDOM."

"Who are you? This is an interesting question because who you think you are influences where you go in life and why you choose to do what you do. It influences your beliefs about what you think you are capable of doing and becoming. There are many factors that combine to help shape who you are as a unique individual—including heredity, culture, socioeconomic background, family, faith tradition, and more—all of which influence the personality you are. So then, who do you think you are?"

—FRANCIS BACON

One way of summarizing this concept is the use of a pyramid—a self-knowledge △ that represents a directional force in your life affecting the decisions you make and how you make those decisions. All the factors that help to shape your self-knowledge △ are quite complex, but a simplification of this concept includes your self-assessed skills, interests, and values. These three components can be defined as follows:

Skills: Your skills are anything you have learned to do well, any special "God-given" talents, or any special aptitudes and strengths you have from early childhood, perhaps from the time of your birth. Skills can include what you are good at, or what you want to be better at. You might have inborn talents that are just waiting for you to practice and perfect them. Education helps bring your strengths to focus. So does volunteer and paid work experience.

Interests: Your interests include anything you do that you enjoy, or anything you have never done that you *would* enjoy doing. Interests are the sparkles of your life—your hot buttons. Press them often and choose to be in environments where they get pressed or where others press them for you.

Values: Your values include anything that is important to you that affects your behavior and what you choose to do, or sometimes not to do. Values are something of worth or importance. They are reflected by your goals—desirable ends that you strive to attain and that provide a sense of purpose to your life.

Of course, testing your stated values against reality is important. For example, perhaps you think it's important (values) to manage or lead other people because your mother is a chief corporate officer in a large company. As a result of this situation, you might "think" you would enjoy (interests) a management-related position. You might also "think" you are good at (skills) leading and influencing people. But after some thought and maybe discussion with your counselor/instructor, you might decide that it's not so important to you after all to be in a managing or leading position. In fact, maybe you begin to realize that you don't really value working with other people, and that you would prefer to work alone in a creative, artistic, and unstructured environment.

The focus here is on *self-assessed* skills, interests, and values—with special emphasis on what you feel is most important to you (your values) and what you enjoy or would enjoy doing (your interests).

The underlying assumption is that if you can discover what you value most in life and what you really enjoy doing, you will be more motivated to learn whatever skills are necessary to accomplish your goals. This approach makes learning and training more relevant. Plus, you already have many transferable skills to use throughout your life journey!

> **IT IS FAR EASIER TO LEARN NEW SKILLS THAT MATCH YOUR VALUES AND INTERESTS THAN TO LEARN NEW VALUES AND INTERESTS TO MATCH YOUR PRESENT SKILLS AND ABILITIES.**

One simple and effective method of clarifying some of your self-assessed skills, interests, and values and identifying your own personal self-knowledge △ is an exercise called "The Banyan Tree." It is divided into several separate but related exercises, so read the directions very carefully, relax, and enjoy the experience!

THE BANYAN TREE

A LITTLE BACKGROUND. . .

In Hawaii there is a very special tree called the banyan tree. These trees are very old and large, often reaching heights of more than 50 feet and usually developing a full branch system that can sometimes expand to fill an area equal to one-third the length of a soccer or football field.

The branches of a banyan tree are so thick with leaves that barely any rain will reach the ground during the brief downpours that Hawaiians refer to as "liquid sunshine." Long vines grow from the branches and hang loosely beneath, providing hours of fun for children who enjoy swinging on them.

On the island of Oahu (sometimes called "the gathering place"), in Honolulu, there are many banyan trees. In one area of the Honolulu Zoo across from Waikiki Beach at the foot of Diamond Head, the leaves of several giant banyans flutter in the gentle trade winds as people stroll by. Below is a map of the area, where there is one very special banyan tree.

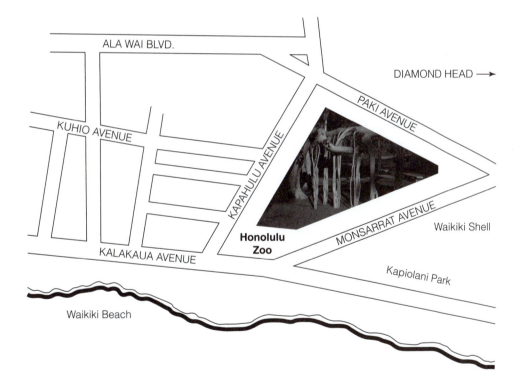

It is here that 50 distinguished people representing different careers from all over the world are assembling. This informal gathering—to celebrate peace, friendship, and an international sharing of ideas—takes place in Hawaii every three years under the same banyan tree. You have been invited to join the afternoon gathering. You are very excited about this event and interested in meeting several of the participants in this international exchange.

You arrive at the banyan tree early, before anyone else arrives. Just as you sit down on the soft, cool grass, a light rainfall fills the air with the sweet scent of wetness. After a few minutes, a spectacular rainbow suddenly appears and seems to end at the edge of the banyan tree just a few feet from where you are sitting. You marvel at how close and real this rainbow is, and you stand up and begin to walk toward it. You imagine what it would be like to really touch a rainbow, to experience "the rainbow connection."

Continue on to the first exercise of "The Banyan Tree," called "The Five-Minute Rainbow Connection."

THE FIVE-MINUTE RAINBOW CONNECTION ®
ADULT DAYDREAMING

This exercise is important because it deals with your fantasies and your dreams, all powered by your imagination. Take your imagination seriously.

Imagine that every child is kissed by an angel at birth and receives an unlimited resource of imagination. During early childhood we reach inside ourselves and touch that resource whenever we want to. The experience is fun, even delightful, and provides us with a source of friendships, exciting places to travel, and unlimited "special" powers.

Then, as we develop and mature over time, something very sad begins to happen. Many of us *think* we lose our imagination. The people around us, the environment, and a combination of factors seem to direct our energies outward. We forget about our inner resources, and we assume we have lost all our imagination.

But angels don't make mistakes! When they touched us at birth, they knew it would last forever. The problem is that *we* don't know that—so we simply shrug our shoulders and say, "I'm getting too old for dreaming" or "I've given up on that stuff—it's only for children."

Not so!

You've still got the same power of imagination inside you that you had as a child. You need only to get into a space for five minutes and rediscover your own personal imagination. It really is there, and it's all yours. Don't be shy, self-conscious, embarrassed, or doubtful. Rather, be daring, expressive, and eager for discovery. Take a chance. You have everything to gain and nothing to loose.

Spend a few a minutes now, and follow these next directions to truly experience "the rainbow connection."

INSTRUCTIONS FOR EXPERIENCING THE RAINBOW CONNECTION

Find some quiet time and "free space" for yourself and relax on a soft, wide chair or on a bed. Close your eyes and breathe in and out five times very, very slowly—inhaling through your nose as much as you can to expand your diaphragm, and exhaling through your mouth, lips almost closed, so that you are blowing the air out, very, very gently. (Take a minute to do your slow breathing now, before continuing on.)

After you feel relaxed, begin to think of yourself as a child about the age of 5 or 6. Imagine yourself playing in an enjoyably relaxing, sunlit, outdoor setting. Imagine yourself to be very content and satisfied. Continue this experience for a minute, and if you begin to find yourself smiling a little, that's a good sign. You're really into it! Simply focus on yourself romping around as a child, enjoying life and doing what makes you feel good. If your childhood was difficult, imagine what it *would* have been like if you did have the opportunity for a more positive and enjoyable experience. Do this for two minutes.

During the final two minutes of this exercise, picture that large, beautiful, colorful rainbow near the banyan tree with yourself approaching the glowing, misty outer edges only 5 feet from you. As you reach out, wanting to experience that unbelievable sensation of really touching a rainbow, to actually feel something no one else has ever experienced, bring yourself up to your present age.

Now focus on the question in the box below. Remember that you are now an adult, not a young child, but you still have the power of the child's imagination in you as you respond to the question.

> **IF TOUCHING THIS RAINBOW WERE SYMBOLIC OF EXPERIENCING SOMETHING I'VE ALWAYS WANTED—LIVING AN AMBITION OR DREAM, BECOMING SOMEONE SPECIAL, OR DOING SOMETHING THAT IS VERY IMPORTANT TO ME THAT SECRETLY I'VE ALWAYS WANTED— WHAT WOULD THAT BE?**

In other words, as you reach out with your heart and mind to actually touch the rainbow, let your imagination create for you the responses to this question. Your responses, in effect, become the experience of touching this rainbow.

Then, as you collect your thoughts and have a clearer understanding of what's in your heart and mind, slowly open your eyes, and write 10 to 12 responses on the blank lines below.

Assume you have all the skills, talents, education, and training to do whatever tasks or activities you specify. Assume you are in prime physical condition and have amazing powers to do anything. Assume you have *total* support and approval from family and friends regarding your choices. Assume you will be *successful*. There are no limits in this list. Have fun—be bold and unbridled with your flow of ideas!

Try to focus on several desired experiences, ambitions, or life dreams. Think about a few of your favorite movies or books and the characters that stand out above the rest. Think about several people, living or dead, whom you admire. Include your favorite heroines and heroes, storybook or TV characters you might want to become, and/or things you have wished for in your heart. Include a few fantasies that could never come true such as, "I wish I could travel in a time machine and go back to early days of dinosaurs." Also include some present-day fantasies that are career-oriented such as, "I wish I could be a successful bed and breakfast owner (or a successful singer, dancer, or famous architect)." Fill 10 to 12 lines.

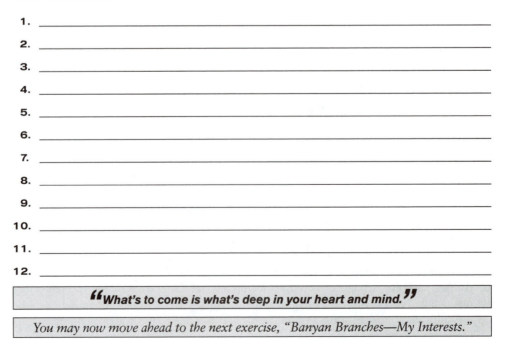

1. _____
2. _____
3. _____
4. _____
5. _____
6. _____
7. _____
8. _____
9. _____
10. _____
11. _____
12. _____

> **"What's to come is what's deep in your heart and mind."**

> *You may now move ahead to the next exercise, "Banyan Branches—My Interests."*

BANYAN BRANCHES—MY INTERESTS

This next exercise deals with your interests—what you enjoy doing or would enjoy doing. Interests are important because they provide the "sparkle" that lights up your life. Everyone enjoys doing some things more than others. It's in our nature as human beings to develop interests as a result of many years of living, exploring, and learning. The six groupings of people described in this exercise represent six primary different areas of interests.

Do not place any notes or marks on this page or fill in any boxes until the directions indicate to do so further on in your workbook.

Below is a view of the space beneath the banyan tree in the Honolulu Zoo. As described in "The Banyan Tree" background, the 50 famous people from all over the world have now arrived and are gathered beneath the tree. These people represent a variety of backgrounds and work experiences and are the best in their fields. They all thoroughly enjoy their work environments. Those who share similar interests have gathered together beneath certain branches of the banyan tree as described below. Each group has been assigned a specific number (1 through 6) that will be the basis for completing "The Banyan Tree" exercises. After a brief discussion, members of each group will be fully engaged in activities that are representative of their specific group.

Read the following descriptions of the different interest groups and then continue on with this activity.

☐ _____

#1 = THINGS The individuals in this group work especially with their hands—operating, building, or repairing mechanical or electrical machinery or equipment. Their work might also include transporting, driving, flying, woodworking, crafts, baking, cooking, or working with computers such as programming or desktop publishing. *In general, the people in this group prefer to deal physically with the environment by working with objects, machines, tools, or even plants or animals (raising them); by cooking and baking food products; or by performing tasks such as producing, transporting, servicing, or repairing.*

☐ _____

#2 = IDEAS The individuals in this group work especially with the mind—observing, learning, diagnosing, evaluating, analyzing, investigating, or solving problems. They might deal with a variety of areas including biology, chemistry, science, medical specialties and technologies, engineering, and architecture. Their work might involve social science–related areas such as psychology, sociology, history, economics, or urban planning. *In general, the people in this group prefer to deal mentally with the environment by using problem-solving and intrapersonal processes dealing with theories, knowledge, or concepts.*

☐ _____

#3 = IDEAS The individuals in this group work primarily with the mind—creating, imagining, or expressing—using visual, written, or verbal approaches, sometimes in innovative, unstructured situations. These people might sketch, draw, or paint. They might play music, entertain others, read, or write poetry. They might create portraits and floral or fashion designs. They might combine written and spoken approaches in such areas as public relations, news reporting, advertising, or directing films. *In general, the people in this group prefer to deal mentally with the environment by using imagination, creativity, and intrapersonal processes dealing with visual, written, or spoken elements, or some combination of these, often in expressive or performance-related approaches.*

☐ _____

#4 = PEOPLE The individuals in this group work especially with people—helping others directly with personal problems or living situations, caring for others, or by ministering, assisting, advising, teaching, or coaching individually or in groups. Their work involves informing, counseling, training, or providing some legal, health, wellness, or cosmetic-related assistance. *In general, the people in this group prefer to deal directly with others through caring and helpful interpersonal processes that provide service or assistance.*

□ _____

#5 = PEOPLE The individuals in this group work especially with people—leading and managing others, overseeing the operations of a project or company, or selling and persuading others to buy a product or take a course of action. Their work might involve law enforcement, education, sales, or management. *In general, the people in this group prefer to deal with others through interpersonal processes, by taking charge and managing or directing them and/or projects, usually with verbal instructions, or influencing others to purchase a product or service.*

□ _____

#6 = DATA The individuals in this group work especially with data—numbers, facts, files, and records. Their work might involve record keeping, accounting, or facilitating the consumption of goods and services. *In general, the people in this group prefer to deal with details, numbers, records, or systematic, impersonal processes such as recording, verifying, transmitting, and organizing.*

> *Review the preceding descriptions of the different interest groups before entering your responses in Box 1 and Box 2 below. Assume you have all the necessary abilities, talents, self-confidence, education, and training, plus the approval of your friends and relatives to support your choice.*

BANYAN BRANCHES INTEREST RANKINGS

BOX 1 □

Which of the six main banyan branches would you visit first, so you could enjoy hearing that group's brief conversation and then *actively participate* in the variety of activities most appropriate for this group based on the description? *Keep in mind that your first choice might be the only group you have a chance to visit—so select the group you feel would really interest you the most.* Write the number of the group that matches your first choice in the box above this question. Do this now before continuing on. Reread the six descriptions if necessary.

BOX 2 □

Alas, after 20 minutes of activities with your first-choice group, an intense downpour of "liquid sunshine" bursts from the sky, and all six groups rush in toward the center of the huge, sprawling banyan tree where no rain reaches the ground. Everyone briefly shares her or his excitement regarding the banyan tree experience—and then suddenly the sun is out shining again.

As the groups gather once more in their respective areas beneath the six main branches of the banyan tree, you discover that your first-choice group has decided to walk across the street onto the soft, warm sands of nearby Waikiki Beach, where they plan a brief swim in the cool, refreshing waters.

However, you prefer to remain beneath the banyan tree and to visit one of the other groups, because you have other interests and would enjoy meeting a different group of interesting people and doing some different activities.

Under which of the five remaining banyan branches would you now most want to be, to hear that group's brief discussion and then *actively participate* in the variety of activities most appropriate for this next group based on the description? *This is the last group you will have an opportunity to be with. Select the group you would most enjoy visiting and doing the various activities most representative of that group.* Place the number of the group that matches your second choice in the box above this question. Do this now before continuing on.

Briefly explain what there is about the *type of people* you would be meeting in each of your first two choices that influenced you to select those groups from among the six possible choices. What interests you most about these people and the activities you would be doing with them?

Reasons for Choice 1 (be specific):

_____

_____

_____

_____

Reasons for Choice 2 (be specific):

_____

_____

_____

_____

_____

Now, on the lines provided below, briefly explain what there is about *you*—the type of person you are—that influenced you to select your first two choices. In other words, you made your selection because you're the type of person who would enjoy . . .

Reasons for Choice 1 (be specific):

_____

_____

_____

_____

Reasons for Choice 2 (be specific):

_____

_____

_____

_____

MY COMMON THEMES

Reread your responses to the above choices. On the lines below, list the *two* different themes you are hearing in your responses. For example, (1) "I see common themes about wanting to be creative and expressing my ideas, perhaps in visual or written formats" and (2) "I notice a theme about observing, learning, and comparing differences among various cultures and lifestyles."

First Theme:

_____

_____

_____

Second Theme:

_____

_____

_____

This exercise has helped you to narrow down six major interest areas to two that you feel are stronger than the others. You may now move ahead to the next exercise, "Banyan Branches—My Skills."

BANYAN BRANCHES—MY SKILLS

Now totally shift your thinking from interests (enjoyment) to skills (ability to do something well). This exercise deals with your self-assessed skills—what you honestly think you're very good at or activities you feel you do very well. Skills are important because being aware of them and using them can produce income. You do some things better than you do others. In fact, you can probably do some activities better than your friends and peers, who just can't measure up to your level of competence. You earn income because others believe you provide the necessary skills and talents to accomplish whatever job needs to be done. No one is going to pay you for doing something you cannot do well. You need to be aware of your skills and talents—and you need to fully believe in yourself.

If you are skilled in specific areas, *but do not believe you are,* others will often agree with your low self-image. Your beliefs about yourself are powerful. Imagine being in an airplane, and the pilot and copilot have suddenly become incapacitated. There is no one available to land the plane! Two people identify themselves as having limited flight training. One is dubious about his training, while the second person indicates a positive attitude about her or his ability to land the plane. Who would you choose to sit in the pilot's seat and attempt the landing?

Most people have hundreds of different skills that they acquired while working in various capacities—whether in the work world or through time spent in an unpaid life role such as volunteering, homemaking, or parenting activities. Most individuals tend to take many of their skills for granted. When asked, "How many skills do you honestly believe you have?" a common response is "Fewer than 10!"

Driving a car is a skill that many people learned, usually as teenagers. Talking to people is a skill that teachers use when they try to motivate their students and excite them about the subject matter, or that news commentators use when they inform us of the day's events. There are hundreds of other examples of skills—ranging from working with your hands and fixing things to being creative and analyzing problems. Even being patient, understanding, and a "good listener" is something many people are good at but take for granted. Being organized, taking charge, and making decisions are all skills that can help you manage large projects efficiently and effectively as well as fun, simple projects like planning a party with your friends.

Some skills are referred to as *innate special abilities*—aptitudes or talents that people are born with. All people have a variety of skills and talents. Many are learned in school and used later in life throughout various career-life roles and are transferred from one job to the next. These *transferable skills* can be used in multiple job changes throughout a person's work history.

There are many young adults who have spent several years in part-time work, school activities, community projects, and hobbies. They have become skilled at a number of activities. Everyone develops a variety of skills, in different areas.

It is important to understand that no one is skilled in all areas. There might be specific areas in which you have many skills, but there are also other areas in which you lack certain skills. That's all right. You can usually learn new skills when you become motivated enough to do so. Motivated individuals are the best learners.

It is possible to divide skills into four major categories: (1) people-related skills, (2) things-related skills, (3) data-related skills, and (4) ideas-related skills. Then it is helpful to self-assess your skill level in each category. For example, compared to your fellow workers or your peers, you might consider yourself above average when it comes to talking with people, managing people, or caring for people. If this is the case, you would rate yourself high in the people-related skills area.

On the other hand, you might be good at working with your hands, making or repairing things, or preparing food. Perhaps you are good at interacting with the physical environment, gardening, outdoor activities, or working with animals. If you consider yourself above average in this category then you would rank yourself high in the things-related skills area.

Looking at your skills relative to these four basic areas can also provide you with some insight about your personality type. The following descriptions of the four basic skills areas include the types of jobs people with those skills would enjoy. Notice how the four areas actually expand into six when considering the two additional categories described under "People" and "Ideas."

PEOPLE skills that involve working directly with others:

1. Helping, teaching, informing, or serving others (examples: counselor, teacher)

2. Selling, managing, persuading, or directing others (examples: sales worker, manager, police officer)

DATA skills that involve working with facts, records, numbers, and business procedures:

3. Recording, checking, or organizing facts and files (examples: accountant, bank teller, office clerk, air traffic controller)

THINGS skills that involve working with objects or tools:

4. Operating, driving, or repairing machines; working with animals or plants; cooking food (examples: firefighter, chef, carpenter)

IDEAS skills that involve working with knowledge, insights, and theories:

5. Solving, diagnosing, observing, or discovering something (examples: scientist, physician, sociologist)

6. Expressing or creating by speaking, writing, or performing (examples: TV news anchor, interior decorator, writer)

The resulting six categories of self-knowledge or personality type are useful for career exploration, and they conveniently fit within the main four areas:

PEOPLE	DATA	THINGS	IDEAS
1. Helping, teaching, informing, or serving others	3. Recording, checking, or organizing facts and files	4. Operating, driving, or repairing machines; working with animals or plants; cooking food	5. Solving, diagnosing, observing, or discovering something
2. Selling, managing, persuading, or directing others			6. Expressing or creating by speaking, writing, or performing

Now, very carefully reread each of the six summaries represented by the six banyan branches on pages 8–9 before responding to this next exercise. This should take about two minutes. You might want to keep rereading some of the summaries as you complete this exercise and decide on your appropriate self-ranking. There might be several areas in which you feel you are skilled or have at least some skills. With reflection, you can probably determine which area generally represents your *strongest* skills.

Next you are going to rank each of the six banyan branches according to how skilled you believe you are in each of the six areas, compared to your fellow workers or peer group. Use the rankings A through F, with A representing your *strongest* skill area and F representing your *weakest* skill area. Use each letter only once.

Place your self-rankings (A–F) on the blank lines to the right of the following banyan branch numbers (1–6) that correspond to your skill estimates. If you're having difficulty ranking yourself compared to your peers, carefully reread the six descriptions and rank yourself based on your perceived level of skill. You may now reread the six banyan branch summaries on pages 8–9 and complete your self-rankings in the left-hand column below.

BANYAN BRANCHES SKILL RANKINGS

#1 _____ (AP; FB; LAP)

#2 _____ (AP; FB; LAP)

#3 _____ (AP; FB; LAP)

#4 _____ (AP; FB; LAP)

#5 _____ (AP; FB; LAP)

#6 _____ (AP; FB; LAP)

Now review your self-assessed skill rankings and circle the appropriate letters in the right-hand column to indicate whether you based each ranking primarily on your *actual performance* (AP), *feedback* (FB) from others who have observed your performance, or simply your own personal opinion with *little actual performance* (LAP). You may circle more than one set of letters if you feel strongly that it is appropriate to do so.

Please do this part of the exercise now before continuing.

Review your skill self-rankings, especially taking note of the basis you used for ranking yourself—that is, whether you relied on your own actual performance (AP), feedback (FB), or little actual performance (LAP). Now, regardless of the original ranking (A–F) you previously indicated, circle only *one* of the banyan branches numbers 1 through 6 that you now feel best matches your *strongest* self-assessed skills area. This might differ from your initial ranking, and that is acceptable.

Remember that counselors, advisors, and instructors can often provide some excellent feedback regarding your strong and weak skill areas. Take some time to discuss your ratings with them when you have an opportunity. Your college or career center might offer special tests that will give you additional information about your specific aptitudes or skill areas compared to your fellow workers or peer group.

You may now move on to the next exercise, "Banyan Branches—Your Values."

"Whether you think that you can, or that you can't, you are usually right."
—HENRY FORD

BANYAN BRANCHES

My Values

> **"It is the language of values that people use to map their world. It is what can inspire them to take action and move beyond their isolation. More often, though, finding the right balance between our competing values is difficult. Our values demand deeds and not just words."**
> —BARACK OBAMA

Once again shift your thinking—this time from skills (ability to do something well) to values (things that are important to you). Values are something of worth or importance, goals, desirable ends that you strive to attain and that provide a sense of purpose to your life. Your values can relate to just about anything you feel and believe is very important to you.

If hundreds of people in a room listed their values, there would probably be hundreds of different specific lists of values, each list with different rankings indicating levels of importance. Some lists of course would be similar, but each of those persons with similar lists of values would most likely have their own personal ranking of what's most important to them.

It is common for people to think their values are "a," "b," and "c," and then experience a partial or total *values shift*. They might discover later on that their values are "b," "f," and "h." Life happens, people respond, then hopefully learn, change, and grow. People's values can shift and change throughout their life journey. Over time, some people discover that some of their strongly held values were not their "true" values. They experience a values shift and discover that several different values are now more important.

For example, for many years you might value working in a very casual environment with flexible hours where you make lots of money—and then wake up one day and realize that money isn't everything, and you desire work with more meaning and purpose. After some reflection, you might eventually decide that you really want to work with young students and be a history teacher.

You might have a secure job in human resources but discover that you are not doing work that is fulfilling. In fact you are stressed and very unhappy. You're not sleeping well and even have frequent migraine headaches. After refection and career counseling, you decide to make a career change. You return to college, become a dental hygienist, and discover work that makes you—and others—smile every day! You have learned that you really value working with people and things (dental equipment) more than with people and data as in your previous work environment.

Perhaps you have a job as a financial analyst where the money is great and the work is okay, but *not* your passion, and you undertake career counseling to clarify your goals. You are very skilled at your job, but you're always dreaming of your secret ideal career—to be a board game creator! So you decide to go for it. In a short time you create eight different board games and sell 100,000 of them. You have learned how to fuel your passion in a part-time ideal career—so you take the leap of faith and devote a full-time effort to your dream job, and your small business takes off!

Finally, maybe you have been a project engineer or construction inspector working on projects valued at millions of dollars. You have always wanted to own your own business, so you try a career shift and start a landscape business. Your main motivator was a realization that you prefer to be independent and spend more time outdoors with hands-on work tasks. But you aren't as financially successful as you thought you would be. You have doubts about your career change and find yourself at a crossroads after several years in the landscape business. You take time to do some career counseling and reflect on your work values. You decide that your career change in fact was the right move—you just need to learn some better marketing techniques and improve your management skills. Soon you have reorganized and expanded your landscape business and are enjoying more success and fulfillment!

All these stories are true—and the same results are possible for you. These stories are about a few of my clients who decided to focus on their values and change their lives for the better. It just takes some time, personal effort, and a willingness to examine yourself, your heart, your present situation, your abilities, your interests, and your true values to discover what gives you a sense of purpose and meaning so you can get your life on the right track.

True values are those that are authentic and very much part of the real fabric of your inner nature—who you truly are. These values are relevant over time throughout your life journey and are less likely to change significantly. They can be hidden for some time as you deal with your life journey and your shifting values. Shifting values are those that do not represent your true nature or who you truly are. They are more prone to change over time. These are "learned" from the influence of others around you (often through *their* values system) or by your experiences with life. Shifting values do influence your beliefs and actions and are often in conflict with your true values.

The values component of self-knowledge is the most important, the most influential, the most challenging to discern. Developing a sense of self and what is truly important takes effort and time because many factors contribute to your complex and ever-developing self-knowledge △. Culture, heredity, the environment, religious tradition, and other factors influence who you are, how you develop, and how you look at yourself. This includes the beliefs you have and the roots of your beliefs.

There is this deep place within you, your core, where your true values, your deep-rooted beliefs, exist. These serve as the cornerstone of your career-life choices. These must be heard, seen, tasted, felt, realized, and clarified for the successful evolution of your life journey.

This is the most confusing part of self-knowledge because values lie deep within a person's heart and mind. It takes lots of deliberation, often causing confusion, to decide what you think is something of worth and very important to you. There are probably many different things in life that you value, and it will be helpful to consider the six banyan branches as one way of grouping different work activity situations that are important to different types of people.

You will find this activity to be challenging and revealing. It will help your shifting values bump up against your true values. Bumps are great in your life journey: They slow you down and cause you to be more diligent and discerning.

Reread the six summaries represented by the banyan branches on pages 8–9 before responding to this exercise. This should take about two minutes. As you read the six summaries, focus on values, and begin to grasp an understanding of how each summary actually describes six different important work activity situations. Ask yourself, "Deep down inside, how important is it for me to be doing these kinds of work activities in my life?"

Remember, do not focus on your skills, and do not let skills (what you are good at) get in the way of values (what's important to you). For example, even though you might be most skilled in the #1 area of the banyan branches (dealing with the physical environment), you might feel strongly that the #4 area (helping and caring for others) represents the kind of work situation you consider to be the most important for you to be doing.

If you find it difficult to separate your thinking from skills, pretend that you are very skilled in all six areas and have all the training and education, even the approval from others, to do any of the activities in banyan branches. Imagine that you *will* be successful in all the six areas! This will help you focus on those areas that you feel are important to you.

> *Reread the six banyan branch summaries on pages 8–9 before continuing on.*

Now it's time to rank your work activity values. Again, use the letters A through F, with A representing the work activity area you feel is *most important* for you to be doing with your life and F representing the work activity area you feel is the *least important*. It is not unusual to find individual statements in several of the summaries that you would want to rank high. However, rank each summary on the basis of the total, *overall* picture you have—especially from the "In general..." statement at the end of each description.

You should decide on your rankings A through F not because *others* have told you these things are important, but rather because *you* strongly feel they are important. Use each letter only once.

Place your self-rankings (A–F) on the lines next to the following banyan branch numbers (1–6) that correspond to the descriptions that represent work activities most valued and those least valued by you. Remember *not* to focus on your abilities, skills, and education or training. Assume that you *will* be successful and have the support of family and friends. Do this now.

BANYAN BRANCHES VALUES RANKINGS

#1 _____

#2 _____

#3 _____

#4 _____

#5 _____

#6 _____

Based on the above rankings, write the letters representing your *top three* ranked work activity areas in the boxes below. (Remember that A is high and F is low. The work activity area that you ranked as A should be placed in Box 1, B in Box 2, and C in Box 3.)

BOX 1 ☐   **BOX 2** ☐   **BOX 3** ☐

Many work situations involve a combination of different work activities, and it is important to think about the combinations you would prefer. The following exercise will help you check the accuracy of your work activity values ratings in the above boxes.

MY IDEAL CAREER SCENARIO

You are going to divide the circle on the next page into pie shapes to represent the amount of time and energy you think is important to devote to the three top-ranked work activity areas you identified in the boxes above. You can choose any combination you want in order to create your ideal work scenario. Assume that you are skilled in all of the six work activity areas.

Divide the circle into three sections, using three different percentages adding up to 100%. Label each section with the appropriate banyan branch number to match your selected percentage.

For instance, in the following example, the division of the circle would indicate that it is important to be spending 60% of your time and energy in #1-related activities, 25% in #2-related activities, and only 15% in #4-related activities:

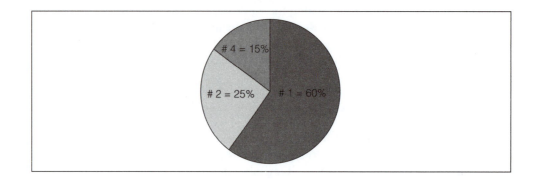

Now divide the Ideal Career Scenario circle into segments that *most accurately* represent the combination of activities you feel is important for you to be doing in your ideal work situation. Review the six banyan branch descriptions on pages 8–9 as needed. Do this now before continuing on.

■ MY IDEAL
CAREER SCENARIO

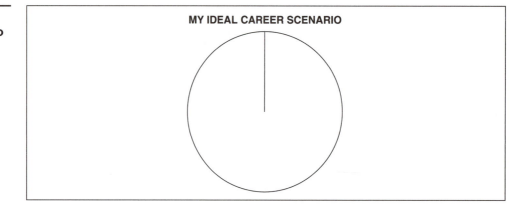

MY IDEAL CAREER SCENARIO

Next, review your top-ranked work activity values in the three boxes on page 17 and *change* your rankings in each of those boxes to match the results of your Ideal Career Scenario circle above. (Remember that A is high and F is low, and the work activity that you ranked as A should be placed in Box 1, as B in Box 2, and as C in Box 3.)

This exercise you have just completed is very important because it deals with your values—more specifically, those work-related activities you feel would represent an ideal work situation for you. The combination you created in the Ideal Career Scenario circle might include some important basic characteristics—but other factors might be missing.

Therefore, on the following blank lines, list *any* characteristics at all—including those represented by the three percentages of the Ideal Career Scenario that you just created—to express more fully your ideal situation. The sky's the limit, so really dare to dream and be specific about what you would most want if you had the power to create your ideal work environment. Some examples might include "the opportunity to work alone" or "the opportunity to travel" or "the chance to earn extra money from overtime or commissions from sales" or "working with a small group of creative colleagues."

Characteristics of My Ideal Career Scenario

1. _____
2. _____
3. _____
4. _____
5. _____
6. _____

Summary Description of My Ideal Career Scenario R&S

After reviewing the specific characteristics you just wrote down as necessary for your Ideal Career Scenario, compose a brief paragraph on the following blank lines that clearly describes what you would be doing in an ideal career situation. To do this, consider all the individual characteristics you have listed and put them together in one brief paragraph that creates a new work situation—totally personalized to fit exactly what you want! This is only a draft and doesn't have to be perfect. Reflect on your Ideal Career Scenario draft and share your description with others as directed by your instructor or counselor.

_____
_____
_____
_____
_____
_____
_____

Before continuing on, compare your results with what you wrote on page 6 as a response to "The Five-Minute Rainbow Connection." You should begin to see some similarities emerging in terms of your interests and values. These similarities are the beginning shape of your self-knowledge △ and the evidence of important life themes common to your life journey and your search for purpose. Sometimes this discovery of self goes against the path set by others or what is expected of you by others. Determining your values and working to achieve them can sometimes be a lonely road—but is always a fruitful one.

> **"It behooves every man who values liberty of conscience for himself, to resist invasions of it in the case of others: or their case may, by change of circumstances, become his own."**
> —THOMAS JEFFERSON

Now let's put together the work you have completed so far in Part I to help you develop a clearer summary of your self-knowledge △.

BANYAN BRANCHES SUMMARY CODES

Review your self-assessed skills, interests, and values as directed below and fill in the appropriate blanks. The resulting summary of self-information should present a clearer picture of who you think you are, what you feel you're good at, what you enjoying doing, and what activities you feel are important for you to be doing in your work role.

SKILLS

Review your Banyan Branches Skill Rankings on page 14 and in the box below write the one banyan branch number you have circled:

(number circled) ☐

INTERESTS

Review your Banyan Branches Interest Rankings on page 9 and in the boxes below write the numbers you have identified as representing your top two choices from this exercise:

BOX 1 ☐   **BOX 2** ☐

VALUES

Review your Banyan Branches Values Rankings on page 17 and in the boxes below write the top three numbers you identified as representing your first, second, and third choices:

BOX 1 ☐   **BOX 2** ☐   **BOX 3** ☐

FINAL SUMMARY CODE

Now look at your Summary Code(s) in a different order—focusing on your values first, then your interests, and on your skills last.

Review your self-assessed VALUES above and write the letter of your top choice in this box: ☐

Review your self-assessed INTERESTS above and write the letter of your top choice in this box: ☐

Review your self-assessed SKILLS above and write the letter of your top choice in this box: ☐

Compare the letters in all the summary boxes for similarities and differences. You should see similarities among the letters for your values and interests and possibly your skills. However, it is not unusual for your skills letter to be different. Many people, because of past work experiences, have skills in areas that are different from what they enjoy doing or consider important to be doing. The letters representing your values and interests are especially important concerning a summary of your self-knowledge △ code.

MY SELF-KNOWLEDGE △ CODE

On the next page is a table that can help you convert your self-knowledge △ code (based on banyan branches 1–6) to the Holland letter code, a tool that might be more appropriate to use with the materials and resources at your college or career center.

BACKGROUND FOR THE HOLLAND CODE AND THE WORLD-OF-WORK MAP

The Holland letter code is based on the research of Dr. John Holland and represents the six personality types described by him. The code letters are R I A S E C and are derived from a self-scoring interest questionnaire called the Self-Directed Search (SDS) created by Holland and used extensively by counselors both nationally and internationally. Holland's research with person–work environment matching is the basis of many popular vocational inventories and CACGSs (computer-assisted career guidance systems) available in most colleges and career centers.

Holland was the ACT (American College Testing Program) vice president for research when he developed a hexagon arrangement of six occupational types. Dr. Dale Prediger then extended the applications of Holland's hexagon and developed the first World-of-Work Map, introduced by ACT in 1973 and updated several times since then, most recently in 2001. The map places occupations into pie-shaped sections of a circle, corresponding to Holland's occupational types. It is based on analysis of several key databases, including ratings of basic work tasks from the Department of Labor and interest inventory scores of more than 200,000 persons in 640 occupations. The most recent version of the World-of-Work Map (see page 52) is used in this workbook along with the Holland code to provide you with a convenient, proven, and effective person–environment matching technology to facilitate your career exploration and help narrow down your choices.

Check with your counselor, advisor, or instructor to identify the written, audiovisual, or computer resources available at your college or career center. If a CACGS is not available, the Holland RIASEC letter codes can be used with other non-computerized resources. Your college will be able to assist you with these.

CONVERSION TO THE HOLLAND CODE

Use the table at the bottom of this page to convert your self-knowledge △ code to the Holland letter code. But first, before converting your own specific scores, take a minute to convert the banyan branch numbers (1–6) on page 14 to the Holland code letters (RIASEC). This can easily be done by turning to the banyan tree on page 7 and placing the Holland letters R I A S E C in the empty boxes directly above the numbers 1 2 3 4 5 6, in a clockwise order starting at the lower left branch of the tree. Do this now, and then continue with your personal conversion score following these four easy steps:

1. In the table below, circle the banyan branch numbers (1–6) that appear in your values and interests summary codes (page 21). You might end up with only one number representing both your values and interests, or two different numbers: one for your values and a different one for your interests. Next circle the corresponding Holland code letter(s) in the conversion table.

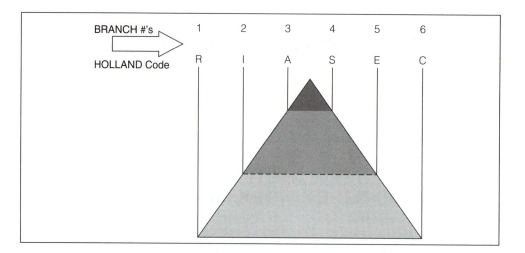

2. Copy the one or two Holland code letter(s) that you have circled, and write those letter(s) into the top part of the large self-knowledge △ in the table.

3. Review the top portion of page 21 (Banyan Branches Summary Codes), and note the numbers in the three boxes under "Values." Circle those same numbers in the conversion table and then circle the corresponding Holland code letters below the numbers, noting the order.

4. Finally, using the order as indicated in the boxes under "Values" on page 21, write the three Holland code letters into the lower portion of the large self-knowledge △ in the table.

Do this now, and continue on for an interpretation of your scores.

REVIEW, REFLECT, RECONNECT : THE HOLLAND CONNECTION R&S

What does your Holland code really tell you about yourself? The Holland RIASEC code is a way of describing your unique personality type. It is a convenient and effective way of examining your self-assessed skills or abilities, interests, and values; evaluating your preferred working style; and showing how your interest patterns are related to specific occupations. The theory and research behind the Holland code indicate that both people and occupations can be described and classified into six different types.

The six Holland types are as follows: (1) Realistic, (2) Investigative, (3) Artistic, (4) Social, (5) Enterprising, and (6) Conventional.

Write these specific Holland types on the blank lines to the right of the Holland letter codes (RIASEC). Follow the order as indicated by the first letter of each Holland type (for example, R = Realistic). Do this now, and then continue on.

The six types use the first letter of each type as a shorthand for that specific type. For example, the Artistic type uses a shorthand of "A," and the Social type uses a shorthand of "S." This way, the six types can be easily referred to as the RIASEC types. This shorthand will be useful when applying the Holland code to the World-of-Work Map to locate job matches later on in your workbook.

Read the descriptions of each type again on pages 8–9, and focus on how each type does appear to have a connection with its specific name, some more clearly matching than others. Overall, these Holland RIASEC code letters with their matching types and descriptions seem to work well as an easy way to describe personality types and matching work environments.

Self-knowledge is one of the most important components of the career-life strategy formula. Developing a sense of yourself takes time. It is not uncommon for adults in their thirties or forties to experience a career-life transition and realize one day that they feel they don't know themselves as much as they thought they did. Yet, after some reflection, these same people will begin to recognize several important themes that run through their career and life histories. Many of these themes often relate to at least one or two of the Holland codes.

Now it's time to discover more clues that you have already written into your workbook based on the activities you have completed so far. You will see one or two main themes emerging, themes that describe the type of person you think you are—your personality type in Holland-coded language.

> *The following is a review of the workbook exercises you have completed in Part I. Read the instructions carefully, and fill in the appropriate blank lines. This will help you identify important themes and prepare you for the rest of your workbook activities, especially those activities that help you discover specific job matches.*

MY CAREER-LIFE THEMES: THE BANYAN TREE EXERCISES

Reread, one at a time, your workbook responses to "The Banyan Tree" exercises, and briefly summarize those responses according to the instructions on the appropriate blank lines.

#1: The Five-Minute Rainbow Connection (pages 5–6)

When you reread your responses to this exercise, you should identify one or two themes emerging from what you have written. For example, perhaps you have described your favorite heroes or imagined situations in which you seem to be helping others or offering your services to others. Your summary might be something like this: "I see myself wanting to spend time with others in a helping, caring way."

Or, perhaps you have described a fantasy situation where you are in charge of a small group of colleagues, collaborating and creating ideas or products that help others. Your summary might be as follows: "I see myself wanting to be in control of a project, coordinating my team, using my imagination to create products or services that will be helpful to consumers."

Remember, what you have already written in response to this exercise is an initial view of your self-knowledge △. Regardless of what you have written or how much fantasy you used, you should still be able to identify one or two emerging themes.

Reread your responses to "The Five-Minute Rainbow Connection." On the lines below, summarize any themes you can identify.

Summary Themes: _____

_____

_____

_____

#2: Banyan Branches: My Interests (pages 7–11)

When you reread your responses to this exercise, try to identify any common themes that are evident. The clues to the themes in this exercise are in the explanations regarding your first two choices. So carefully review what you have written as reasons for your first and second choices and note what you have indicated under "My Common Themes" on page 11.

Summary Themes: _____

_____

_____

_____

_____

#3: Banyan Branches: My Skills (pages 12–14)

When you review your self-ratings on this exercise, note two clues. First reflect on the one banyan branch number you circled that indicates your top-ranked self-assessed skill area. Also note the two skills areas you marked with an A or B rating. If any of this information matches the top ratings in your interest rankings or values rankings, that's good. You seem to have some self-assessed skills in areas where you also have interests and values. On the lines provided below, write a brief summary of your top two rated skills.

If your skill rating does not match your interests and values, or if you feel you are not skilled in any of the six categories, don't be overly concerned. You now know what skill areas you might want to develop further in order to do those things you enjoy and you feel are important to be doing. Therefore, on the blank lines below, also write a brief summary describing the skills you most want to develop in the future.

Summary Themes: _____

_____

_____

_____

_____

#4: Banyan Branches: My Values (page 15–20)

When you reread your responses to this exercise you should identify the major themes that are emerging from your summary description of "My Ideal Career Scenario"—the brief paragraph you've already completed on page 18. Briefly summarize those themes on the lines below.

Summary Themes: _____

_____

_____

_____

    Congratulations! You have worked hard at identifying clues and themes about yourself and how you look at yourself. Look for evidence of these themes throughout your workbook. Based on your review and written summaries of the exercises in Part I, you should be seeing some emerging similarities regarding your interests and values, which should be reflected in your self-knowledge △ code.

    The most important task at this stage in your workbook is to identify and understand any similarities and differences. You should be noting more similarities than differences right now. However, you might find some differences you don't understand, and you can discuss these with your counselor, advisor, or instructor.

    Remember, there are many factors that contribute to your emerging self-knowledge △. The work you have completed in Part I is an important beginning—a starting point from which you will be creating some of your career-life directions.

    Turn to Appendix 1 on page 91 to locate "My Main Summary Themes: #1, #2, and #4." Write the one or two *main* themes emerging from a reflection of your summary themes in the activities you completed as follows: #1 The Five-Minute Rainbow Connection (page 4); #2 Banyan Branches: Your Interests (page 7); and #4 Banyan Branches: Your Values (page 14). After you have filled in this section of Appendix 1, continue with this workbook.

> *Please continue on to the next self-paced section, Part II, to learn about some important and powerful concepts regarding career-life decisions.*

> **"Twenty years from now you will be more disappointed by the things you didn't do than by the ones you did do. So throw off the bowlines. Sail away from the safe harbor. Catch the trade winds in your sails. Explore. Dream. Discover."**
>
> —MARK TWAIN

PART
II

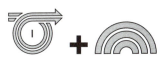

KEY CONCEPTS FOR MAKING SUCCESSFUL CAREER-LIFE DECISIONS

Part I of *Creating Careers with Confidence* focused on *you*—your self-assessed skills, interests, and values. You reviewed the basic career-life strategy and identified your personal self-knowledge △ code—your Holland code that is a summary of who you think you are. You will be using your Holland code in Part IV, when you begin to locate occupations in the World-of-Work Map that match your code. You will also apply this same code to those non-work career-life roles into which you also put much time and energy throughout your life journey.

Many people will have 7 to 10 jobs in a lifetime, but work is only one of a variety of roles you play in your life. It is a critical role, of course, because you earn needed income from your work—but other roles are also important to your life journey, your well-being, and the well-being of others, especially those close to you.

Part II will focus on three important concepts that provide an effective framework for improving all your career-life decisions—including work and non-work roles—and are especially applicable to your academic decisions. These concepts are easy to understand and can be positive and powerful forces in your life. All you need to do is apply them!

The first concept deals with understanding the reflective and intuitive processes of decision making. This is one of the main components of the career-life strategy formula and is represented by a circular symbol that looks a bit like a donut with an arrow on top and an important **I** in the center representing your "inner eye"—your ever-present, highly intuitive true self that assists you with career-life decisions throughout your life journey.

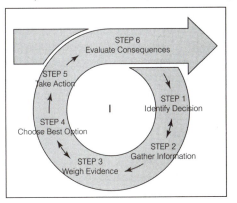

The second concept involves the various roles you play in life. It is also one of the main components of the career-life strategy formula and is represented by a series of rainbow bands, each signifying a different career-life role. It is important to achieve a sense of balance across your career-life roles.

The third concept describes the interplay between different personality types and work environments. It emphasizes the importance of understanding how your personality might fit into a specific environment and how certain person–environment matches can be more satisfying to you than others. A final discussion will integrate all these ideas to provide a framework for your improved career-life decisions and directions.

After completing Part II, you will be better prepared to examine the world-of-work. You will learn how to identify occupations that best suit you, to create career-life scenarios that are fulfilling and financially rewarding, and to discover paths that provide a sense of purpose and meaning.

THE REFLECTIVE-INTUITIVE DECISION-MAKING PROCESS

Life always involves making choices. You make most of your decisions by yourself—many automatically without a lot of deliberation. Sometimes you allow others to make decisions for you. That can be a conscious or a subconscious choice. There are usually more choices available than immediately appear, and you are usually in a position to make the final decisions about most things that affect you.

Some of the choices you face have serious consequences and are difficult to make. The more serious the potential consequences to you, the more you need to know how to make wise and informed decisions. The process illustrated here is a carefully integrated combination of reflection and intuition and can help you make wise choices resulting in positive consequences for yourself and others. Much of the wisdom you will gain during your life evolves from decisions you make regarding your daily personal experiences and how you make choices. Monitor your choices to discover life themes.

> **"Life is the only real counselor; wisdom unfiltered through personal experience does not become a part of the moral tissue."**
> —EDITH WHARTON

Reflective Decision Making

Reflective decision making is designed to slow down your deliberation and encourage you to stop and think—to carefully consider options before making your final choices. It consists of six steps that, when followed, produce very satisfying results. This process is most useful with decisions that involve serious consequences for you or others close to you.

Quickly read the six steps outlined in the illustration on the previous page, and imagine the time it would probably take to use this process. Remember that you would want to use this process for decisions that have serious consequences, so you most likely would be willing to spend the time necessary to achieve positive results from your deliberation. There are usually many variables to consider with most major decisions, and taking time to fully review your decisions with all their complexities is valuable.

Intuitive Decision Making

Intuitive decision making is usually more immediate, but it can also assist you with decisions that have serious consequences. Using your intuition means applying your personal inner compass, handcrafted and shaped with the richness and complexity that only *your* life experience could create. Your intuition helps you decide rather spontaneously what to do or what not to do under pressure. It is often very accurate.

With an accumulation of life experiences over time, you can train yourself to listen and discern more effectively, so your intuition is more readily accessible. However, be careful *not* to rely solely on your intuition for complex decisions that involve a lot of variables. The reflective process is essential when you are deciding complex issues. The intuitive process is best used under pressure when you don't have the benefit of time for deliberation and careful evaluation, and you need to act very quickly.

Combining Both—The Reflective-Intuitive Approach

In actual practice, you can use both reflective *and* intuitive decision-making processes in tandem. Many of your serious career-life decisions will involve multiple variables, and the reflective process should be the preferred strategy for your overall approach to arriving at decisions of this type. But don't put your intuition out of sight! Keep it in the waiting area, to be used appropriately *during* the reflective process.

The reflective process is more deliberate, involving multiple steps that enhance the possibility of a positive outcome. It is especially appropriate for career-life decisions that require looking at various alternatives, gathering numerous pieces of information, and weighing evidence to determine the best ways to narrow down and choose the best option. The reflective process takes time and thought, and that is its very nature: It's *reflective*. But you can always apply your intuition at any time as you progress through the six steps, to double-check your feelings and see how your heart (intuitive process) and mind (reflective process) are in sync. Using both processes, within the overall context of the reflective process as presented in this workbook, will be most useful for many of your serious career-life decisions. Hence the name *reflective-intuitive*.

A Word About Impulsive Decision Making

Many decisions you make don't have serious consequences and therefore do not require a structured reflective or intuitive approach. You can simply "go with the flow" and be carefree. These impulsive decisions are not guided by deep-seated intuition, thoughtful deliberation, or reflection. They are influenced more by how you are feeling in the moment—and that feeling could change in the next moment.

Impulsive decision making is useful and enjoyable in many of life's situations where the consequences are not serious. For instance, a common impulsive decision-making experience occurs at ice cream shops as you read about the numerous flavors, toppings, and cone types and sizes. You don't undertake a long process to make up your mind—you simply choose what sounds good at the moment.

> BUT WHAT IF YOU USED THE REFLECTIVE-INTUITIVE
> PROCESS TO BUY AN ICE CREAM CONE?

"THE ICE CREAM CONE": APPLYING THE REFLECTIVE-INTUITIVE PROCESS

The six steps of the reflective-intuitive decision-making process are illustrated in the following example. (Normally, of course, it would be more appropriate to rely on impulsive decision making to buy an ice cream cone. It's easier, more enjoyable, has the hint of adventure, and doesn't keep people waiting for hours in line behind you!)

You might want to follow along using the illustration on page 29 as the steps are described.

STEP 1: IDENTIFY YOUR DECISION Become aware of the specific decision you want to make.

Example of a decision to be made: *You are tossing a Frisbee with your friend at the local park about 11 a.m. and tell her you are hungry and think you want some ice cream or some other snack. You tell your friend you'll be back shortly because the snack shop is just around the corner. Your decision is: What should you buy to satisfy your hunger?*

If you were relying exclusively on the intuitive process, you would move directly from Step 1 to Step 5—having covered Steps 2, 3, and 4 intuitively, quickly, and subconsciously to arrive at a point where you felt comfortable about what you eventually end up doing in Step 5. But in this example you are also going to use the reflective process in your decision. (Of course the impulsive process is best for ice cream purchases, and you would most likely have already *impulsively* selected an ice cream cone before even reaching this point!)

STEP 2: GATHER TWO KINDS OF INFORMATION TO IDENTIFY OPTIONS To identify your options, you will need two kinds of information: self-knowledge information and world-of-options information. In this case, the world-of-options will be the "world-of-ice-cream-and-snack-food." Examples of self-knowledge information: *What flavor do you want? How many scoops would you like? Do you want your ice cream in a cone or in a cup? Do you prefer toppings or plain ice cream? What other food might you like? How much money do you have to purchase your ice cream and other food? Should you buy a snack for your friend?*

Example of world-of-ice-cream-and-snack-food information: *What ice cream flavors are available? What types of cone are available? What cup sizes are available? What toppings are available? What other snack food is available? What are the costs of these options?*

STEP 3: WEIGH EVIDENCE TO NARROW OPTIONS Evaluate the quality of several person–options matches to narrow down those that seem to best match your self-knowledge information.

Example of weighing evidence: *You are very hungry. You have $5, and one small cone costs $1.75. If you have two scoops, the cost would be $3, and if you add two toppings the cost would total $3.50, leaving you with $1.50. A small bag of chips would cost $1.50. You love toppings, and could eat two scoops easily. You could also buy a small bag of chips to eat with your ice cream cone. Your friend might like to be surprised with an ice cream treat. If you get only a small cone you could buy a second one for your friend and still buy a small bag of chips to share. That would make her very happy.*

STEP 4: CHOOSE THE BEST OPTION Select the best option based on your final evaluation of self-knowledge and world-of-ice-cream-and-snack-food information.

Example of choosing based on the final evaluation: *You decide to buy two one-scoop cones with no toppings and a small bag of chips to share with your friend. You know you are very hungry and could easily eat two scoops and the small bag of chips, but you think your friend would like to be surprised with an ice cream treat, and you would definitely feel great surprising her.*

STEP 5: TAKE ACTION REGARDING YOUR SELECTED OPTION Do something appropriate that supports your decision, moves you toward your goal, and allows you to achieve it.

Example of taking action: *You purchase two one-scoop cones with no toppings and a small bag of chips to share with your friend. You go back to the park and surprise her with the ice cream and chips.*

STEP 6: EVALUATE YOUR DECISION AND ITS CONSEQUENCES Evaluate the results of your decision and the consequences, so you can apply this information to future decisions.

Example of reviewing your decision and the consequences: *You did surprise your friend and she was very happy. She loved the ice cream cone, especially because you picked her favorite flavor, Mocha Almond Fudge Delight. You felt great that you were able to surprise her. You lucked out with selecting her favorite flavor! (You guessed.) You probably should have asked her, before you left the park, if she wanted to come along with you to the snack shop. She did not want any of the chips, and you got to eat the whole bag yourself! This turned out pretty good. Next time you'll have a larger breakfast or bring $10 to the park.*

HOW REFLECTIVE-INTUITIVE DECISION MAKING WORKS

Making decisions about career-life situations is much more complicated than deciding whether to buy two scoops of ice cream or go for the "share with a friend and hope for the small bag of chips" plan. The following discussion examines how the reflective-intuitive process works with many career-life decisions you will face throughout your life journey. Each step is discussed in detail to provide you with a comprehensive understanding of the process involved and its importance and relevance to your decision making.

Remember to use all six steps for decisions that have serious consequences. As you progress through the steps, you should simultaneously and spontaneously apply your intuition to double-check your feelings against the more deliberate reflective process. This approach effectively balances the use of careful and deliberate reflection with your ability to tap into the deep well of your inner guidance and stay on course.

Step 1: Identifying Your Decision

This process of making decisions places responsibility directly on *you*. Especially at Step 1, you are the only person who can agree to begin doing something about where your life is headed.

Many students often experience school without asking themselves some key questions related to why they are enrolled, where they are headed, and what they are headed for. Many other people live their lives without asking themselves these *why, where,* and *what* questions.

So although being in Step 1 might be only a first step, it is a crucial first step that gets you involved with the decision-making process. As you can see in the graphic of the reflective-intuitive decision-making process on page 29, Step 1 is the entrance to the entire process. By moving yourself into Step 1 you are, in a manner of speaking, getting into orbit around the decision to be made. If you aren't in orbit around your decision, you are in some other space and time. It will be difficult for you to focus on your decision, let alone make a wise and informed one.

Once you are aware of the need to make a specific decision, you are off to a good start. You are also more motivated because you have focused your attention and feelings on something you are ready to deal with. It is important to be very specific at Step 1 and clearly identify the decision to be made For example, you might be asking yourself, "Should I choose this major, or that one?" Or perhaps your decision is whether to pursue one career or another. In either case the decision is about which of your options will be the best choice. An important follow-up question is, "What do I *want* to do?" A "want" statement is a more focused values statement.

You might now find it beneficial to move immediately to Step 2 so you can start to collect the necessary self-information about your values, interests, and skills or abilities to further assist with the decision to be made. You also need to collect information about your options in order to examine them sufficiently and be able to move to Step 3 and identify alternatives. The more effectively you complete Step 2, the easier time you will experience with all the other steps.

Step 2: Gathering Two Kinds of Information to Identify Options

There are basically two types of information to be gathered at this step to help you identify options. These are (1) self-knowledge information and (2) relevant information about the world-of-options you are considering—such as the world-of-college-majors or the world-of-work—to discover specific occupations. In addition to collecting these two types of information, you must also be prepared to sort out and process the information you have gathered.

This is important information to consider, and the time you spend at Step 2 is the key to making wise and informed decisions throughout your life. *Skip this step and you have indeed made a decision to let time and chance take charge of your life and make decisions for you.* Oh yes, your life will move on and you with it, but you will experience your life as a hit-or-miss journey without you in the driver's seat. This can be a frustrating and debilitating experience, and life will be a drag. Worse yet, without you in the driver's seat, there's a good chance you might go off the road with tragic results.

It is impossible to make wise and informed career-life choices throughout your life without spending sufficient time at Step 2. Unless you understand who you are and especially what you want, you will not often make good decisions for yourself on a consistent basis, even with great intuition. That's because most major career-life decisions involve many details that you must sift through, with attention to multiple variables.

To effectively use your self-knowledge △, you must first have accumulated or collected sufficient self-knowledge information about who you are, what you enjoy, what you are good at, and what's important to you in life. You already have sufficient self-knowledge information because you have been accumulating this over time as you mature and simply experience life. Most people have enough self-information to make initial career-life decisions by the time they are in their late teens or early twenties. They continue to expand on that self-knowledge base as they experience more of life through playing their many career-life roles, especially through education and work.

> **IF YOU AREN'T IN ORBIT AROUND YOUR DECISION, YOU ARE IN SOME OTHER "SPACE AND TIME." IT WILL BE DIFFICULT FOR YOU TO FOCUS ON YOUR DECISION, LET ALONE MAKE A WISE AND INFORMED ONE.**

Once you've taken the time to accumulate enough self-knowledge, you need to be ready, willing, and able to process, sort out, and deal with that knowledge. Many adults who have lived life and accumulated enormous amounts of self-knowledge are afraid or unwilling to honestly look inside themselves and deal with that self-knowledge. Other times, they might be willing to deal with their self-knowledge—but, because of external pressures such as unemployment or divorce, they cannot effectively process it. These external or internal pressures often prevent a clear view of self, and not being *ready* to process self-knowledge translates into not being *able*.

You might find that gathering information about the world-of-options you are considering—for example, college majors, career paths, or specific occupations—is a relatively easy task compared with collecting self-knowledge information, which requires more reflection and soul searching. For this reason you will probably spend more time gathering and understanding your self-knowledge information. However, both types of information are vital components of Step 2, and having one without the other places you in a frustrating position because you probably won't be able to identify or narrow down your alternatives. You need both.

The optimal result that occurs at the completion of Step 2 as you match your self-knowledge information with world-of-options information is the identification of appropriate choices for further consideration. (You will continue to evaluate and further narrow down these options at Step 3.) Most importantly, remember that the real success of your efforts at Step 2 is based on the accuracy of your self-knowledge information. Take the time to reflect, ponder, deliberate, and challenge yourself. This will contribute to successful career-life exploration and planning experiences.

Step 3: Weighing Evidence to Narrow Options

This step requires some critical thinking and evaluation, as you analyze and narrow down the options you identified as potential choices in Step 2. You will need to rely heavily on your self-knowledge △, especially your values, to effectively weigh the options before making a final choice in Step 4. The goal of Step 3 is to narrow down your options to those *preferred options* that are clearly the "finalists" that you will take to Step 4, where you make your final choice—your decision. This is also an excellent time to use your intuition to better "feel" where you are and how you like what you have completed so far in the process. This use of intuition to assess your progress is very important.

Step 4: Choosing the Best Option

This step *is* your decision. To make your final choice, you will again rely on your self-knowledge △, especially your values. You might also want to close your eyes for a moment at this point and use your intuition as a final double-check before moving on. This works!

Step 5: Taking Action Regarding Your Selected Option

It is possible to complete all of the steps of this excellent reflective-intuitive decision-making process through Step 4 and go nowhere at all—if you don't take action. *Not taking action is itself a decision.* Some people do exactly this and end up frustrated. Taking action is important. If you have completed all the steps from 1 through 4 and are satisfied with your progress, you are ready for Step 5. This action step should occur very easily and will most likely produce your desired outcome. So now is the time to trust the effort you put into Steps 1–4, and *just do it!*

If you truly feel something is *not* right at this point, stop and review your efforts at the previous steps. That's the beauty of this process, as you can see in the illustration on page 29, you can easily move forward or backward from Step 1 though Step 4, right up to Step 5. But once you implement Step 5, there's no going back. You've taken action.

If you don't get the desired result, you might need to make a new and different decision at this point. But don't worry. You're back to Step 1, so just move forward once again.

Step 6: Evaluating Your Decision and Its Consequences

This step is often done intuitively and subconsciously. You either feel good about where your decision has moved you, or you don't. However, it is also useful to consciously assess your decisions. This will help you make better decisions throughout your life journey.

If you experience positive consequences, that's great. You've made a wise, informed, and reflective decision.

If you experience negative consequences such as discomfort, restlessness, or anxiety, you might need to make a new and different decision, one that can move you away from negative consequences. It is useful, however, to sit awhile in your discomfort zone because change often brings discomfort. Do not to make a rash decision at this time. First reflect and recycle back into Step 1—but this time, identify a new decision.

And this is the beauty of such a decision-making process. It is reusable and never wears out. In fact, the more you use it, the better you get at using it, and it begins to fit in naturally with your entire way of experiencing your life journey.

One important task for all your decision making is to evaluate the decision you are making and decide whether it might have serious consequences, or relatively unimportant consequences. If you can do this, you are off to a great start! As stated earlier, the reflective-intuitive decision-making process is appropriate only for decisions that might have serious consequences for you or others close to you. For decisions that have less serious consequences, such as selecting an item on a dinner menu or choosing a new pair of dress slacks or a blouse—and of course buying an ice cream cone—you might not want to be so deliberate. Being impulsive for that type of decision making will probably add some excitement to your daily routine!

> **"Do, or do not. There is no 'try.'"**
>
> —YODA (*THE EMPIRE STRIKES BACK*)

THE CAREER-LIFE CONCEPT

Now that you understand the reflective-intuitive decision-making process, a second concept that you can apply to your personal career-life decisions is called the *career-life concept*. As you read about this concept, you might want to ask yourself about specific decisions that you need to be making in the various career-life roles as they are presented. Your workbook will prompt you to consider this question at the appropriate time.

One way of viewing the term *career* has been to focus mainly on work-related activities. This perspective is viewed by most informed people as one-dimensional and restrictive. A more richly relevant, dynamic, and expanded definition of *career* has emerged, replacing the traditional "What I do from 9 to 5, pays me bucks, and hopefully I like it" paradigm. The expanded definition still takes into account the work activities you experience throughout your life—but it is all-encompassing and includes activities you experience in your other non-work roles. Some examples are being married and/or spending time with your friends (the Spouse/Friendship role), raising a family (the Parent role), spending time with your favorite hobbies and fun activities (the Leisurite role), and attending classes to earn a degree (the Student role).

Even experiencing a divorce and becoming a single parent can have major implications for you in this more relevant understanding of *career*. Your work-related activities are important and provide income to support your basic needs, selected lifestyle, and personal and family goals. For many, work takes up a major portion of their days, weeks, and entire lives. In fact, when some people retire, they might become depressed and need a reorientation to the rest of their life roles. Many people are used to working and sometimes feel lost without their jobs, their routine schedules, employment settings, and coworker relationships.

You are, have been, and always will be involved in other-than-work activities, and these activities often overlap. You do many of these different activities daily, and they are important to you and take up much of your time. Thus, your career becomes expanded to other areas of your life, not just the work area. The term that more effectively describes the variety of activities you experience from day to day across different roles is *career-life*, implying the sum of all the activities in which you are involved over time or at any one time in your life.

Several people began to discover this new paradigm shift in the late 1970s. I started using the term *career-life* when I was working with a group of women enrolled in a career planning course that I was asked to teach in Hawaii in 1976. It was part of a new federally funded program designed for "displaced homemakers"—women in transition who had not previously attended college and needed a fresh start in life. After a few classes, I realized how limiting the traditional concept of career planning was for these women, and changed the focus to "career-life exploration and planning" to accommodate their rich lives and the stories they each brought to this class. I began to share this paradigm throughout Hawaii with my undergraduate students and in counselor education programs where I taught.

Several years later, I met a lifelong mentor, JoAnn Harris-Bowlsbey, who informed me that Donald Super, an eminent career development theorist, had also been focusing his work on this new paradigm. He had developed an enjoyable and unique way of explaining this concept by using a rainbow to represent a person's various life roles. He placed his emphasis on the "life" aspect and called his rainbow a *life-career* rainbow.

I have always preferred the term *career-life* and use a series of pyramids overlaying someone's self-knowledge △ to represent different life roles into which people attempt to play out their lives and express their skills, interests, and values. This workbook will refer to the rainbow as the *career-life rainbow*.

Super played a key role in creating and refining the new career-life paradigm, and his basic concepts and poetic and colorful rainbow are emphasized in this workbook. Super's rainbow shows that people, as they develop, take on increased responsibility and can often play a variety of "roles" in many "theaters." The major roles and the primary theaters in which they are played, according to Super, are as follows:

Life-Career Roles

- Child (son/daughter)
- Student
- Worker
- Spouse/friendship
- Homemaker
- Parent
- Leisurite
- Citizen
- Annuitant

Life-Career Theaters

- Home
- Community
- School
- Workplace
- Retirement (community or home)

Let's further explore Super's rainbow to get a clearer understanding of what the different roles really mean and how they can often blend together. (As you read, refer to the illustration on the next page.) Super's life-career roles are described as follows:

Child (Daughter/Son) Your relationship to your parents or guardians and the time and energy spent in that relationship

Student The time and energy spent in education or training at any time in your life

Worker The time and energy spent in work for pay at any time in your life

Spouse/Friendship Your relationship with your husband, wife, life partner, or someone very close to you and the time and energy spent in it

Homemaker Time and energy spent in taking responsibility for home maintenance and management

Parent Your relationship with your children and the time and energy spent in that relationship

Leisurite The time and energy spent in leisure or spare-time activities

Citizen The time and energy spent in civic, school, church, or political activities

Annuitant The role that replaces worker—that is, the time in life when you will receive Social Security, pension, or other types of retirement income

When we place each of these roles on rainbow bands, one role per band, the career-life rainbow begins to take shape. The person's age begins at birth on the left and continues, as the person ages, around the arc to the right. The shaded areas of the rainbow bands indicate time and energy spent in each particular role. Each role that is played takes up a certain amount of time and energy. As more roles are played, more time and energy will be required. A brightly colored rainbow indicates strong, positive, emotional involvement and balance among various career-life roles. Paleness or a spotted band indicates those life bumps that challenge us and often take the wind out of our sails. We then feel stuck and can more easily drift off course.

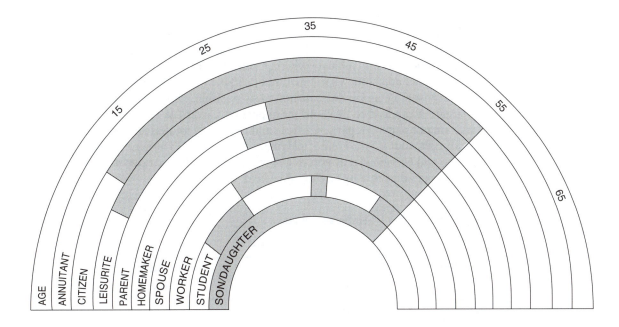

Let's explore the career-life rainbow of an imaginary person at age 55, as illustrated below. As can be seen, at age 20 the imaginary person is playing several roles at the same time. These roles include child (daughter/son), worker (just beginning), leisurite (with sports and a coin collection), and citizen (helping at a local soup kitchen for the homeless once a week). All these roles are occurring on or just beginning at age 20. Notice that the student role (age 6–20) has just ended, but only temporarily, and the leisurite and citizen roles have been active since childhood. At age 35, in addition to the roles just mentioned, the same person has now has activated the student, spouse, homemaker, and parent roles—all being played at the same time! And although the student role continued for about three years before ending, it was being played again beginning at the age of 50. At age 55, this person is playing eight roles!

By looking at Super's rainbow, you can understand why he defines the term *career* as the combination and sequence of all the roles played by a person during the course of his or her lifetime—many often played or experienced at the same time.

Now is a good time to review your own rainbow and the career-life roles you are presently playing. You will better understand "what's going on" and "what's not going on" in your life and how you feel about it. This will be a good starting point before dealing with your future. In other words, taking a good look at your *present* situation first will put your planning about your *future* into the proper context.

Enjoy the next exercise as you evaluate your present career-life rainbow.

EVALUATING MY PRESENT CAREER-LIFE ROLES R

Review the various career-life role definitions on pages 38. Read each of the following roles and circle any of the major roles you are presently playing. Make sure you circle both "present age" and "early childhood" under the child role if appropriate. Next, under "Satisfaction Level," indicate whether you are very satisfied (VS), fairly satisfied (FS), or unsatisfied and somewhat frustrated (US/SF) with each role by circling the appropriate response. Be as candid and honest as possible. Only your openness to your present situation can lead to new and more positive career-life directions.

If you are not playing a particular role and are happy and satisfied not playing that role, it's all right. But if you are not playing a role and you feel you really want to be putting time and energy into it, you might want to indicate your dissatisfaction in not being able to play that role by circling the US/SF option.

Major Roles	Satisfaction Level			→
Child (present age)	□ VS	□ FS	□ US/SF	_____
Child (early childhood)	□ VS	□ FS	□ US/SF	_____
Student	□ VS	□ FS	□ US/SF	_____
Worker	□ VS	□ FS	□ US/SF	_____
Spouse/friendship	□ VS	□ FS	□ US/SF	_____
Homemaker	□ VS	□ FS	□ US/SF	_____
Parent	□ VS	□ FS	□ US/SF	_____
Leisurite	□ VS	□ FS	□ US/SF	_____
Citizen	□ VS	□ FS	□ US/SF	_____
Annuitant	□ VS	□ FS	□ US/SF	_____

Now go back to the blank spaces under the arrow to the right of each role and enter the appropriate letters IFC (I freely choose) or IBO/C (influenced by others or by circumstances) to indicate whether you are playing each role because you freely choose to become as involved as you are or whether you are spending time and energy because you are influenced by others or by circumstances to do so. Once again, be as candid and honest as possible.

Do this exercise now before continuing on. If you are not playing a particular role and really want to be, indicate IFC or IBO/C on the blank lines.

Now continue with the next exercise, "My Personal Career-Life Rainbow."

MY PERSONAL CAREER-LIFE RAINBOW

You are now ready to work on your personal career-life rainbow. First, briefly review the major roles you are presently playing and your degree of satisfaction with these roles, as indicated in the previous exercise. Next, color or shade with crayons or colored pencils a 1-inch area at the point of your approximate age in each of the bands on the blank rainbow at the bottom of this page. A bright, intense shade (lots of color) would represent strong positive emotional involvement, while a lighter pale shade or even tiny dots (little color) would represent less positive emotional involvement with that particular role. Feel free to use the same color for all the bands or a different color for each rainbow band. Use a pen or pencil if no crayons are available. Remember, this exercise should represent how you honestly feel about your *present* career-life situation. (You will have an opportunity to work on your future career-life situation later on.) Your colored-in rainbow should accurately reflect your personal satisfaction ratings when you evaluated your career-life roles in the preceding exercise. You may color or shade in your personal career-life rainbow now.

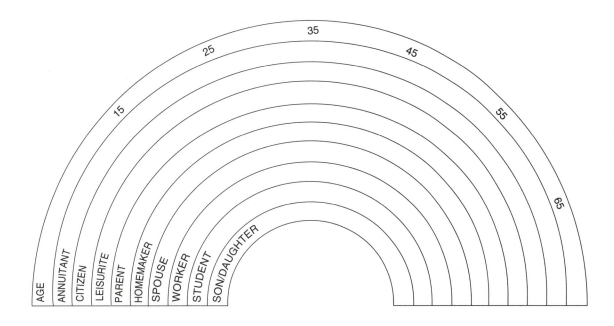

Turn to Appendix 1 on page 91 to locate "Evaluating My Present Career-Life Roles." Complete activity A by writing your one main reason for each role you rated as FS or US/SF in the space provided. Then complete activity B by writing your insights regarding how best to deal with difficulties you experience in various roles. It might be helpful to talk with an appropriate person, such as a counselor, to discuss any concerns that you have regarding your present career-life situation or any recurring themes, including ways of responding to difficulties across various life roles.

ABCs FOR A VIBRANT AND SUCCESSFUL RAINBOW

As you better understand the many career-life roles you are playing in your life, the following guidelines can help you with the creation and nurturance of your personal career-life rainbow. Think of them as your ABC's for success.

A: Adjust as Necessary Monitor your career-life rainbow at least weekly, to make needed adjustments in the time and energy you are putting into your various roles. A brief 1-minute end-of-day silent reflection can provide important insights, reduce stress, and help you set realistic, achievable goals.

You will sometimes be overextended and play too many roles—or you might not play enough roles to give your life balance and fulfillment. Taking on new projects and responsibilities or dealing with unplanned emergency situations will challenge your entire rainbow equilibrium and could upset whatever balance you had previously experienced and enjoyed. Self-monitoring through daily mini-reflections can keep you on track and help you get back on track when derailed.

B: Be Sensitive Learn to be sensitive to how and why your roles affect your other roles as well as the career-life roles of people close to you. Put effort each day into seeing life and situations of those close to you through their eyes. Learn to express empathy effectively and without attachment to your ego and your own defenses.

Each role you play will have some impact on your other roles and the roles of your significant others—spouse, children, parents, relatives, friends, and coworkers. When you are more aware of the dynamics involved between your own rainbow and others' rainbows, you are better able to share empathy with those around you who are experiencing their own challenges. Sharing empathy strengthens your own capacity for dealing with personal life challenges.

C: Create a Balance Create a balance in your career-life rainbow that blends the roles you *need* to play with the roles you *want* to play. Recognize the difference between the two, accept responsibility for doing what needs to be done, and passionately and intentionally engage life by setting goals, achieving them, and experiencing a sense of purpose.

Most major difficulties you will have in your life journey involve bumping into unmet expectations—both those you set for yourself and those that others have set for you. Learn to examine your own motives for thinking, judging, believing, and behaving. Earnestly and honestly evaluate the difference between career-life roles you *need* to play (whether influenced by others or by life circumstances) and those roles you truly *want* to play. Life is not perfect, and sometimes not fair—at least in the short run. Deal with this. The one thing that no one can take from you is your own *capacity to respond* to any challenge, any difficult person, or any life situation. As you gain more clarity about what you *need* to deal with and what you *want* to deal with, you will experience fewer feelings of disappointment and frustration over both the former *and* the latter. (Now that is *real* freedom!) This will open your heart and mind with an authentic willingness to receive—and you can achieve the measure of goodness that life does in fact have specifically for *you*.

> **"In the attitude of silence the soul finds the path in a clearer light, and what is elusive and deceptive resolves itself into crystal clearness."**
>
> —MAHATMA GANDHI

PERSONALITY-ENVIRONMENT MATCHES R&S

John Holland has developed an important concept that is useful in career-life exploration and planning. Basically, the principal elements of Holland's theory match personality types with corresponding environments and then explain behavior based on the interaction of personality and environment.

In other words, Holland states that a person of a given personality type would be most satisfied working in an environment that matches, supports, or nourishes that particular personality type. Likewise, a person of a given personality type would most likely be *unhappy* working in an environment that does *not* match, support, or nourish that personality type.

Holland believes that cultural and personal forces—for example, parents, social class, culture, and the physical environment—shape people in different ways. Out of these experiences, a person learns to prefer some activities above others. Later, with reinforcement from parents and others, the preferred activities become strong interests, leading to the development of skills or competencies. Finally, a person's interests and competencies create a personal disposition that leads to thinking, perceiving, and acting in special ways—and all these factors combine to help create who a person really is.

Holland also believes that this developmental sequence is continuous from childhood to adulthood and evolves over time depending on the environments encountered. Obviously, some environments will be more or less supportive of a person's development than others.

Holland's research indicates that most people can be categorized as some combination of six personality types, with greater dominance in two or three types, and that most environments can also be similarly categorized into some combination of six types. Holland believes that most people tend to surround themselves with others like themselves who share their interests, competencies, and outlook on the world. Where people congregate, they create an environment that reflects those qualities. People search for environments that will allow them to exercise their skills, interests, and values.

As described in Part I, the Holland code is a convenient way to learn more about your interests, examine your values and self-assessed skills, and discover the best person–work environment matches for you.

All the exercises you completed in Part I of your workbook relate to your personality type. The six descriptions in The Banyan Tree relate to Holland's six personality types and similar work environment types.

The following exercise will help you review your self-knowledge △ code, develop a brief summary statement about your code that reflects your personality type, and discover a potential environment that can best suit your personality type. You will need to go back to certain exercises already completed in your workbook and fill in the appropriate blank spaces as directed.

MY PERSONALITY TYPE

Review your self-knowledge △ code on page 24. Then in the boxes above, enter your top three code letters using the Holland letter codes (RIASEC) that are written in the lower half of the large pyramid at the bottom of that page.

Now review "My Career-Life Themes" on pages 26–27 and on the lines provided below briefly describe your personality type as reflected in your various summary themes—specifically #1, #2, and #4. In other words, if your Holland letter codes are AEI, and your summary themes reflect this code, you might write the following:

"I enjoy creating ideas and using my imagination, perhaps with words, music, and some visual effects, to promote concepts and influence others. I especially enjoy interacting with small groups of three to five with me serving as a project coordinator. I also enjoy learning about what motivates people."

_____

_____

_____

_____

_____

_____

MY ENVIRONMENT TYPE

Review what you have written under "Summary Description of My Ideal Career Scenario" on page 19, and on the following blank lines summarize the environment you created for yourself in that exercise. Try to be as specific as possible—almost as though you were describing the environment to someone who has never known or experienced such an environment.

_____

_____

_____

_____

_____

_____

Now reread your environment summary above and, using the six descriptions in The Banyan Tree (pages 8–9), select the two or three Holland code letters (RIASEC) that best reflect your ideal environment as you have described it. Enter the letters in the empty boxes above, to the right of the heading "My Environment Type."

The Holland codes you just identified in the previous exercise and this one—and wrote in the boxes next to "My Personality Type" and "My Environment Type"—should be very similar. They might match exactly, although this is not necessary. At least two of the three Holland code letters should appear in both sets of boxes.

You might want to check with your counselor or instructor if your personality and environment codes do not match at all. It is important for you to discover environments that match your personality type. In this way, your environment can nourish you and allow for more self-expression.

Turn to Appendix 2 on page 93, and follow the directions under "My Ideal Career Scenario #1—Draft 1." Then continue with this workbook.

A FRAMEWORK FOR IMPROVED CAREER-LIFE DIRECTIONS

Donald Super's career-life rainbow and Holland's personality–environment match are similar in focus and also quite compatible. Together, they provide an important theoretical framework for your career-life decisions. Following is a summary of their key points:

- Who you think you are will be reflected in where you choose to work and live. Your career-life choices are, in fact, implementations of your self-concept.

- The developmental sequence of your experiences over time and the way your interests develop, grow, and seem to flow from your life history and your personality are important influences in determining who you are.

- The choice of an occupation is an expressive act that reflects your abilities, interests, values, and other "personal determinants," as Super calls them, such as aptitude and biological heritage.

- Culture, social class, home, community, school, and other "situational determinants," as Super calls them, shape you in different ways over time and combine to create a particular disposition—a way of thinking, perceiving, acting, and choosing what roles to play in preferred environments or "theaters" of life.

Thus, who you are, as shaped by a variety of factors over time, has a lot to do with what environments you find most satisfying and what roles you choose to play within these environments. Likewise, the environments you search for that satisfy you and the roles you choose to play affect each other and have an influence on you, your career-life decisions, and the people close to you with whom you often interact.

If you consider yourself, as well as your skills, interests, and values, along with other factors such as heredity, disposition, and personality traits (in general, who you are)—and use a $\triangle$ to represent all this—you could refer to this as your self-knowledge $\triangle$. Considered this as a sort of building block, cornerstone, or perhaps a directional energy force in your life. This energy must be released to achieve happiness.

The environment around you—including socioeconomic factors, culture, home, school, friends, and community—can be represented by the career-life rainbow, each band symbolic of a specific environment in which you might be playing a role. These roles allow you to express yourself and release the energy that is inside you.

Most roles you play are chosen by you. Other roles you play are selected for you, and you agree to continue playing them. There are some roles you decide not to play at all, or that you are prevented from playing.

Your self-knowledge $\triangle$ is the main influence that helps you select the roles you play in your environment. It also influences how you cope or do not cope with certain roles that you might find yourself playing from time to time even though you did not select them. What influences how you choose to play various roles? How does this affect you state of happiness?

The most important factor—values—is at the base of your self-knowledge $\triangle$. Your value system directs you to move mountains in life, becomes your inspiration for everything you do, and acts as the cornerstone of your self-knowledge $\triangle$.

The better you understand yourself, especially your values, the more opportunities you will have to play a variety of satisfying career-life roles throughout your life, contribute your talents to others, and experience happiness.

The concepts you studied in Part II are powerful and can have a strong influence on how you complete this workbook. They can be used for all your future career-life decisions. Reread any section in Part II that might need clarification.

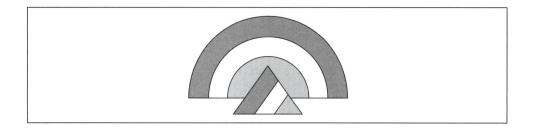

"If you want happiness for an hour—take a nap. If you want happiness for a day—go fishing. If you want happiness for a month—get married. If you want happiness for a year—inherit a fortune. If you want happiness for a lifetime—help someone else."

—CHINESE PROVERB

You may continue on to Part III to learn about the next important component in the career-life strategy called "The World-of-Work."

PART

III

THE WORLD-OF-WORK:
WHERE THE JOBS ARE!

There are more than 20,000 occupational titles and 12,000 occupations from which to choose, and emerging occupations always present new opportunities and new challenges, especially in a global economy. The average 27-year-old has already held seven jobs, and most people will eventually have as many as 10 different jobs in at least two or three different career fields. Many jobs are *bridge jobs*—jobs that allow you practice and learn new skill sets before using them to "bridge," or move to another job. A job transition might result in increased income, more responsibility, or enhanced job satisfaction. You transfer your learned skills and move vertically or horizontally along your career path. How do you choose wisely from the overwhelming selection of possibilities?

Self-knowledge is important when making career-life decisions. But knowledge of the world-of-work and how it is organized is also important for applying your self-knowledge. Without understanding how the world-of-work is organized, even with sufficient self-knowledge, searching for occupations would be a confusing and difficult task because there are so many choices. Fortunately, occupations do share certain common characteristics.

THE WORLD-OF-WORK MAP

One effective way of understanding the world-of-work and how occupations are related to one another has been developed by Dr. Dale Prediger and the American College Testing (ACT) Program. This tool was introduced in Part I and is called the World-of-Work Map.* This circular, pie-shaped arrangement is organized in several ways to help people understand how easy it is to conceptualize the entire world of work with its thousands of occupations. First, specific occupations are positioned into the W-o-W Map according to their relationship to four work basic task areas that represent occupations that have opposite work tasks and are subsequently placed opposite each other: People, Data, Things, and Ideas, (see Part I). Then, the four work tasks actually expand into six "clusters" that roughly correspond to Holland's six occupational types (see Part I). Furthermore, the W-o-W Map also divides the six clusters occupations into 12 "regions" of work, which contain 26 specific career areas, each career area representing many related occupations. If all this seems a bit confusing, refer to the World-of-Work Map on page 52.

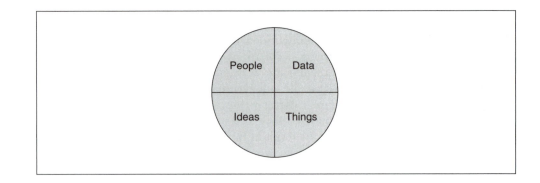

Now try the following activities, in which you will use the World-of-Work Map to indicate your work preferences.

---

*The World-of-Work Map, 3rd edition, is copyrighted by the American College Testing Program, Iowa City, IA, 2001. All rights reserved and used with permission.

MY WORK TASK PREFERENCES

All work tasks can be classified according to the primary purpose or focus of those tasks. The four main categories of work tasks are People, Data, Things, and Ideas. These actually expand into six categories, because the people-oriented and ideas-oriented work environments can both be expanded to create two additional categories:

PEOPLE work environments that involve tasks like these:

1. Helping, teaching, informing, or serving others (examples: counselor, teacher)

2. Selling, managing, persuading, or directing others (examples: sales worker, manager, police officer)

DATA work environments that involve tasks like these:

3. Recording, checking, or organizing facts and files, numbers, or business procedures (examples: accountant, bank teller, office clerk, air traffic controller)

THINGS work environments that involve tasks like these:

4. Operating, driving, or repairing machines, objects, or tools; working with animals or plants; cooking food (examples: firefighter, chef, carpenter)

IDEAS work environments that involve tasks like these:

5. Working with knowledge, insights, and theories in order to solve, diagnose, or discover something (examples: scientist, physician, sociologist)

6. Expressing or creating by speaking, writing, or performing (examples: TV news anchor, interior decorator, writer)

The resulting six categories of work environments below relate to the six similar categories of self-knowledge or personality types that you learned about in Part I and conveniently fall within the main four areas:

PEOPLE	DATA	THINGS	IDEAS
1. Helping, teaching, informing, or serving others	3. Recording, checking, or organizing facts and files, numbers, or business procedures	4. Operating, driving, or repairing machines, objects, or tools; working with animals or plants; cooking food	5. Working with knowledge, insights, and theories in order to solve, diagnose, or discover something
2. Selling, managing, persuading, or directing others			6. Expressing or creating by speaking, writing, or performing

Review the World-of-Work Map below and circle the major one or two work tasks—People, Data, Things, or Ideas—that *interest* you the most. Limit your choices to only one or two. Reread the work task descriptions if necessary to help you select your favorite choice(s). Do *not* choose based on your skills or education. Assume you have the necessary skills, training, and education to do the activities, including the total support and encouragement from others such as family and friends.

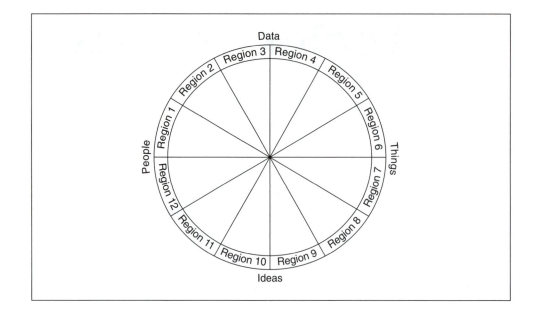

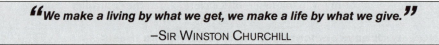

"We make a living by what we get, we make a life by what we give."
−SIR WINSTON CHURCHILL

MY WORLD-OF-WORK REGIONS PREFERENCE

As stated earlier, the World-of-Work Map organizes the four basic work tasks (People, Data, Things, and Ideas) according to 12 "regions," as you can see in the illustration in the preceding exercise. Each region deals with some aspect of the four basic work tasks, or some combination of them.

The breakdown below shows how combinations of work task preferences relate to corresponding world-of-work regions. Review each work task preference grouping, and circle the *one* that best and most accurately matches your preferred work activities. Also circle the corresponding world-of-work region(s). For example, if you feel that you are mostly a "people person" and prefer people-related work activities, you would circle People and the corresponding region (12 and 1). If you are basically a "people and data person" and prefer activities that involve a combination of people and data, you would circle People/Data and the corresponding region (2).

Indicate your world-of-work regions preference now.

Work Task Preferences	Corresponding World-of-Work Regions
People	12 and 1
People/Data	2
Data	3 and 4
Data/Things	5
Things	6 and 7
Things/Ideas	8
Ideas	9 and 10
Ideas/People	11

Now go back to the World-of-Work Map from the previous exercise and use a crayon or pencil to shade in the World-of-Work region(s) that you identified as corresponding to your preferred work task grouping. In Part IV, you will be able to identify which World-of-Work Map regions closely match your Holland code.

EXAMINING THE WORLD-OF-WORK MAP

Now it's time to examine the entire World-of-Work Map. As you read, turn to the illustration on page 52 to better understand the discussion.

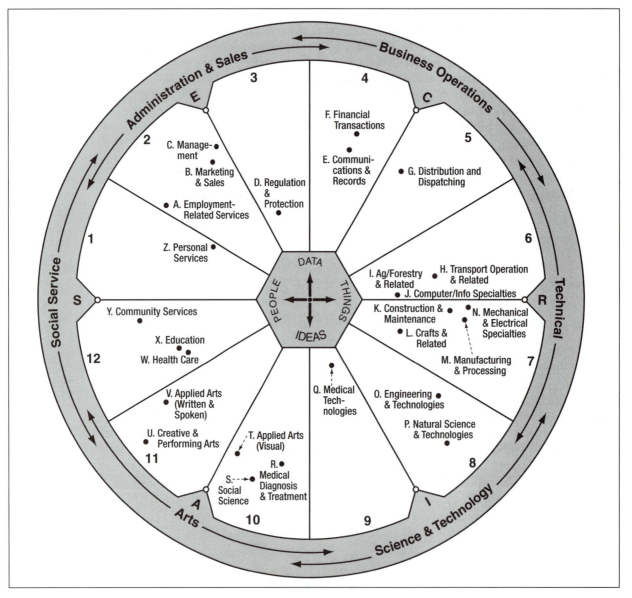

Notice that the six general "clusters" of work (Social Services, Administration & Sales, and so forth) and the related Holland types (RIASEC) are shown around the shaded outer edge of the map for easy reference. Occupations have also been classified into 26 career areas depending on their relation to the four main categories (People, Data, Things, and Ideas). The career areas are represented by little dots (·), and each has a specific name. Each career area is a "home" for hundreds of similar jobs, which makes it much easier to locate jobs that match your interests, skills, and values. Together, the 26 career areas cover all U.S. jobs.

Most jobs in a career area are located near the point shown, although some might be in adjacent regions. Because they are more strongly oriented to people than things, two career areas in the Science & Technology cluster (Medical Diagnosis & Treatment and Social Science) are located toward the left side of the map in region 10, rather than in region 9 where you might expect to see them.

The six general types of work (career clusters) and related Holland types (RIASEC) are shown around the outer edge of the map. The overlapping career cluster arrows indicate overlap in the occupational content of adjacent career clusters.

Career areas that are located close to each other on the World-of-Work Map share similar relationships with certain work tasks—people, data, things, or ideas. Career areas that are very different are located on opposite sides of the map. For example, career areas F and E deal mainly with data and are located close together in region 4. Career areas R, S, and T deal mainly with ideas and are located together in region 10.

To see how certain occupations fit into specific career areas, locate career area N (Mechanical & Electrical Specialties) in region 7. The occupations in this career area involve mostly *things*—jobs such as avionics technician, dental laboratory technician, or auto body repairer. The position of career area N is logically positioned in the Things side of the map at the far right side of region 7. This is called the Technical career cluster and is the Holland code R as indicated on the shaded outer edge of the World-of-Work Map.

Now locate career area Y (Community Services) in region 12. The occupations in this career area mostly involve *people*—jobs such as school counselor, social worker, or lawyer. The position of career area Y is positioned in the People side of the map at the far right side of region 12. This is called the Social Service career cluster and is the Holland code S as indicated on the shaded outer edge.

The World-of-Work Map thus organizes many occupations into a logical, easy-to-understand arrangement. Knowledge of the world-of-work is an important component of the career-life strategy formula. You now understand how the world-of-work can be divided into logical sections, or pieces of the pie. When you use this information to narrow down your career choices in Part IV of this workbook, you will be directed to appropriate resources, including Internet sites that will provide excellent job search and labor market information. This labor market information includes salary, demand and supply estimates, job outlook, important demographic considerations, and much more.

> **"Where in the world is Matt Lauer, Carmen Sandiego, and these jobs . . . ?"**
> —E. A. Colozzi

A WORLD-OF-WORK MAP
MINI-QUIZ

Before continuing ahead, take two minutes to test your understanding of the World-of-Work Map, how it is organized, and where and why certain occupations are positioned. Follow the directions and have fun with this mini-quiz.

On the blank lines to the right of each occupation, indicate the correct career area in which that occupation belongs. Refer to the World-of-Work Map on page 52 for assistance and reread any section in Part III to help you discover the correct answer. You may do this exercise now.

Occupation	Career Area Letter
Machinist	_____
Social worker	_____
Recreation therapist	_____
Graphic artist	_____
Dental hygienist	_____
Architect	_____
Registered nurse	_____

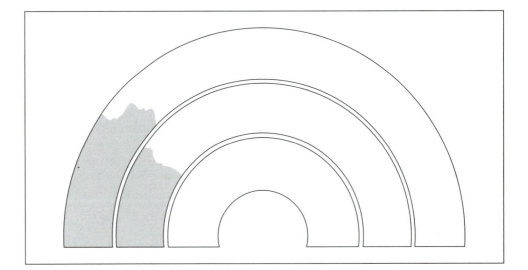

You may now continue on to Part IV, which will bring together all the components of the career-life strategy formula and help you identify occupations that best match your Holland code. To check your answers on the brief mini-quiz, look ahead to the title of Part IV. The correct career area letters on your mini-quiz should match the first letter of each word in the title of Part IV.

PART IV

MATCHING YOU WITH THE WORLD-OF-WORK

Now it's time to match your Holland code with the World-of-Work Map. Review your Holland code on page 24 the three-letter Holland code in the bottom portion of your large pyramid. Your college or career center will most likely have resources and materials compatible with the Holland code letters (RIASEC).

Write your three-letter Holland code on the blank lines below using the appropriate letters (RIASEC):

My Holland code is _____ _____ _____.

USING MY HOLLAND CODE TO MATCH WORLD-OF-WORK REGIONS AND CAREER AREAS

The first thing to do is narrow down your choices from the hundreds of possible careers and occupations—to zero in on those that most closely match your interests, skills, and values.

NARROWING DOWN MY CHOICES

In the table at the bottom of this page, circle the three letters of your Holland code in the left-hand column. Indicate the ranking (1st, 2nd, or 3rd) of your three code letters on the blank line next to each letter, in the column labeled "Ranking."

Circle the world-of-work regions that match your code letters. Finally, review the World-of-Work Map on page 52, and write the specific career areas (lettered A–Z) that interest you. You might also want to compare your responses to this exercise with your responses to a similar exercise you completed on page 53 (matching your work task preference with corresponding world-of-work regions) as well as your results from any interest inventory you took or any CACGS you might be using.

You have narrowed down the world-of-work to specific regions and career areas that seem to be a closer match to you. The following activity will help you identify specific career clusters and actual occupations that correspond to your Holland codes.

IDENTIFYING SPECIFIC CAREER CLUSTERS AND CAREER AREAS

This next activity has three steps that are easy to follow. Your hard work and your attention to detail are now going to bring you results. This should all come together for you like a puzzle that you've been working on that finally starts to make some sense.

For now, put aside any concern about your skills, your abilities, or your education level. These *are* important concerns and will be addressed later on. For this activity, however, focus on where your *heart* is leading you.

Step 1

Write your *top three* ranked Holland code letters (RIASEC) here:

#1 _____   #2 _____   #3 _____

Now review the Holland code letters below and circle the letters that are your *first two* choices as indicated by #1 and #2 above. Note the main work tasks (People, Data, Things, or Ideas) that match your *top two* Holland code letters. Circle them in the right-hand column.

Code		Ranking	Regions	Career Areas (A–Z)
R	=	_____	6 and 7	_____
I	=	_____	7, 8, 9, and 10	_____
A	=	_____	10 and 11	_____
S	=	_____	12, 1 and 2	_____
E	=	_____	2 and 3	_____
C	=	_____	3, 4, and 5	_____

Code Letters		Related Work Tasks
R = Realistic	......	Things
I = Investigative	......	Ideas
A = Artistic	......	Ideas
S = Social	......	People
E = Enterprising	......	People
C = Conventional	......	Data

Step 2

Circle your *top three* Holland code letters and the matching career clusters below:

Code Letters		Matching Career Clusters
R = Realistic	......	Technical
I = Investigative	......	Science & Technology
A = Artistic	......	Arts
S = Social	......	Social Service
E = Enterprising	......	Administration & Sales
C = Conventional	......	Business Operations

Step 3

Review the career clusters and career areas in the chart on page 54 and place a check beside any of the six career clusters and 26 career areas (A–Z) that match your three circled Holland code letters in Step 2.

MY MOST INTERESTING CAREER CLUSTERS

Review the six career clusters in Step 3, and on the blank lines below list the clusters you checked (for example, Administration & Sales or Science & Technology) that interest you the most.

_____

_____

_____

■ CAREER CLUSTERS AND CAREER AREAS (A–Z)

ADMINISTRATION & SALES CAREER CLUSTER

A. Employment-Related Services Manager (human resources, training/education, employee benefits, etc.); recruiter; interviewer; job analyst.

B. Marketing & Sales Agent (insurance, real estate, travel, etc.); buyer; sales/manufacturers' representatives; retail sales worker; telemarketer.

C. Management Executive; executive secretary; purchaser; general manager (financial, office, property, etc.); specialty manager (retail store, hotel/motel, food service, etc.). *Other managers are in career areas related to their work.*

D. Regulation & Protection Inspector (customs, food/drug, etc.); police officer; detective; park ranger; security manager; guard.

BUSINESS OPERATIONS CAREER CLUSTER

E. Communications & Records Receptionist; secretary (including legal and medical); court reporter; clerk (order, billing, hotel, etc.).

F. Financial Transactions Accountant/auditor; cashier; bank teller; budget/credit analyst; tax preparer; ticket agent.

G. Distribution & Dispatching Shipping/receiving clerk; warehouse supervisor; mail carrier; dispatcher (flight, cab, etc.); air traffic controller.

TECHNICAL CAREER CLUSTER

H. Transport Operation & Related Truck/bus/cab driver; locomotive engineer; ship captain; aircraft pilot; sailor; chauffeur.

I. Agriculture, Forestry, & Related Farmer, nursery manager; pest controller; forester; logger; groundskeeper; animal caretaker.

J. Computer & Information Specialties Programmer; systems analyst; information systems manager; computer repairer; desktop publisher; actuary.

K. Construction & Maintenance Carpenter; electrician; bricklayer; tile setter; painter; plumber; roofer; firefighter; custodian.

L Crafts & Related Cabinetmaker; tailor; chef/cook; baker; butcher; jeweler; silversmith; handcrafter.

M. Manufacturing & Processing Tool and die maker; machinist; welder; bookbinder; printing press operator; photo process worker; dry cleaner.

N. Mechanical & Electrical Specialties Mechanic/technician (auto, aircraft, heating/air conditioning, electronics, dental lab, etc.); repairer (office machine, appliance, TV/VCR, CD player, etc.).

SCIENCE & TECHNOLOGY CAREER CLUSTER

O. Engineering & Technologies Engineer (aerospace, agriculture, nuclear, civil, computer, etc.); technician (electronics, mechanical, laser, etc.); surveyor; drafter; architect; technical illustrator.

P. Natural Science & Technologies Physicist; astronomer; biologist; statistician; soil conservationist; food technologist; crime lab analyst.

Q. Medical Technologies (*also see area W*) Pharmacist; optician; prosthetist; technologist (surgical, medical lab, EEG, etc.); dietitian.

R. Medical Diagnosis & Treatment (*also see area W*) Physician; psychiatrist; pathologist; dentist; optometrist; veterinarian; physical therapist; audiologist; physician assistant.

S. Social Science Sociologist; experimental psychologist; political scientist; economist; criminologist; urban planner.

ARTS CAREER CLUSTER

T. Applied Arts (Visual) Artist; graphic artist; photographer; illustrator; floral/fashion/interior designer; merchandise displayer.

U. Creative & Performing Arts Writer/author; musician; singer; dancer; music composer; movie/TV directors; fashion model.

V. Applied Arts (Written & Spoken) Reporter; columnist; editor; advertising copywriter; public relations specialist; TV announcer; librarian; interpreter.

SOCIAL SERVICE CAREER CLUSTER

W. Health Care (*also see areas Q and R*) Administrator; recreational therapist; psychiatric technician; dental hygienist/assistant; geriatric aide.

X. Education Administrator; teacher; aide (preschool, elementary, secondary, special education, PE, etc.). *Other teachers are in career areas related to their specialty. For example, physics teacher would be in area P.*

Y. Community Services Social service director; social worker; lawyer; paralegal; home economist; career counselor; clergy.

Z. Personal Services Waiter/waitress; barber; cosmetologist; flight attendant; household worker; home health aide; travel guide.

MY MOST INTERESTING CAREER AREAS

Review the 26 career areas (A–Z) in the chart on page 60. On the blank lines below, write the career areas letter (A–Z) and specific area names you checked that most interest you. Beside each selected career area, write any of the sample occupations for that area that also interest you. For example, in the Administration & Sales career cluster, career area A is Employment-Related Services, and two occupations in that area are recruiter and job analyst.

Career Area Letter	Career Area Name	Specific Occupations of Interest
(example) A	*Employment-Related*	*Recruiter, Job Analyst*

You now have a good idea of the career areas and occupations that most closely match your Holland code. You may continue on to the next exercise, "My Two-Step Safety Net."

MY TWO-STEP SAFETY NET

It is often wise to have a *safety net* in certain situations during your life journey—even if you are confident in your efforts and feel you are on track. This is one of those situations. You have worked hard to reach the point where you are now and have done a great job of narrowing down the world-of-work based on lots of reflection and a thorough examination of self-knowledge and the structure and organization of the world-of-work. You have successfully identified a list of preferred occupations based on matching your Holland code to the world-of-work options as evidenced in the preceding exercise.

Now it's time to use your safety net. It is important to do this simple exercise to double-check your efforts. You will feel much better having completed it, as you then move forward to complete this workbook.

As you do this exercise, focus only on your interests (what you enjoy) and values (what is important for you to be doing with your time and energy)—*not* on your abilities or training. Imagine that you have all the necessary skills, abilities, training, education, and self-confidence to do any of the jobs you review. Also assume that you have the total approval from people close to you, including family and friends. *This is very important to keep in mind as you do this activity.* Reread this paragraph while you are doing the activity when you feel yourself focusing on skills, ability, and any lack of education or training. This is normal—so simply refocus on your interests and values.

STEP 1: CIRCLING OPTIONS

First turn to page 60 and review *all* six career clusters, *all* 26 career areas (A–Z), and *all* the sample occupations listed for each career area. As you review this information, circle *any* career cluster, *any* career area (A–Z) and *any* occupations of interest, including the clusters and career areas you already checked in the previous exercise. *Put aside any concern about your skill or ability to perform. Focus only on your interests and values.* If you are not familiar with a specific occupation and would like some descriptive information, refer to the *Occupational Outlook Handbook* (OOH). This informative resource is published by the Bureau of Labor Statistics, an agency of the U.S. Department of Labor, and is available online (www.bls.gov/oco).

Circle any occupation that gets your attention and sparks your interest—regardless of ability needed, your age, your sex, or any other factors. Do this now before continuing on.

STEP 2: NARROWING OPTIONS

You might find that most of the occupations you circled fall within a cluster, career area, and World-of-Work Map region to match your Holland code. That's good. Some might not, and that's also good. This activity is designed to help you better understand why you might have circled certain occupations that don't match your Holland code.

Under the appropriate headings below, list those occupations you circled that *do* and *do not* match your Holland code.

Occupations I Circled That *Do* Match My Holland Code:

1. _____

2. _____

3. _____

4. _____

5. _____

6. _____

7. _____

8. _____

9. _____

10. _____

Occupations I Circled That *Do Not* Match My Holland Code

1. _____

2. _____

3. _____

4. _____

5. _____

6. _____

7. _____

8. _____

9. _____

10. _____

PERSONALITY–ENVIRONMENT MATCHES

One way of better understanding which occupations seem to fit the type of person you are is to observe the various World-of-Work Map regions where your preferred career areas are located and determine the logical fit of your personality–environment match.

When Occupations *Do* Match My Holland Code

Review the occupations you listed (in Step 2) that *do* match your Holland code. Use the chart on page 60 and the World-of-Work Map on page 52 to assist you with this activity. On the World-of-Work Map, circle the specific career areas (A–Z) that correspond to the occupations you listed in Step 2. Also note the regions and the major work tasks (People, Data, Things, and Ideas) that correspond to your preferred career areas and regions. There should be a logical match between the specific occupations you listed and the corresponding career areas, regions, and work tasks.

For example, let's assume your Holland code is S—dealing with people in a helping or servicing manner. If you have listed social worker or recreational therapist, notice how those occupations seem to logically fit into the parts of the World-of-Work Map, as follows:

Social Worker	**Recreational Therapist**
Career area = Y	Career area = W
Region = 12	Region = 12
Work task area = People	Work task = People
Career cluster = Social Service	Career cluster = Social Service

You can easily see that the major work task area (People), the career cluster (Social Service), and the region (12) are all the same. Only the career areas (Y and W) are different. There are logical similarities between both occupations because of the type of people contact and service to others. The match between these occupations and your Holland code (S) is logical. In fact, as seen on page 60, there are several career areas in the Social Service cluster that would match your S code—specifically career areas W, X, Y, and Z.

As you review all the occupations you listed in Step 2 that *do* match your Holland code, you will see the personality–environment matches that exist for many of your choices. Complete your review now before continuing on.

When Occupations *Do Not* Match My Holland Code

Now review the occupations you listed in Step 2 that *do not* match your Holland code. A quick review of page 60 will help you identify which career areas and clusters contain occupations that *do not* match your Holland code. For each of the occupations you listed that *do not* match your Holland code, ask yourself what might be the main reasons for your interest in that occupation. You will find that most of your main reasons can be easily matched back to your Holland code, even though the occupations themselves *do not* match your code.

For example, if your code is S (Social) and you listed the occupation of receptionist (career area = E; region = 4; work task area = Data, and career cluster = Business Operations), you might have listed that occupation because of its involvement with people. Receptionists do help people and assist them—but that occupation is not represented by the Holland code S because receptionists mostly deal with Data work tasks and are logically represented by the Holland code C. You should think twice before considering such an occupation if your first or second Holland code is S. There might be too much data involvement in such a job and not enough involvement directly assisting others. The job might not be a good fit for you. Reread the descriptions for Social and Conventional on pages 25–27 under "The Banyan Tree" in Part I to fully understand this distinction.

As you review the occupations you listed that *do not* match your Holland code, you will begin to see that a personality–environment match *really does exist* because of your reasons for initially being interested in that specific occupation. Beside each occupation you listed in Step 2 that *does not* match your Holland code, write the one or two letters of your Holland code that seem to best correspond to the *main reasons for your interest in that occupation.*

For example, if your interest in that occupation is based mainly on helping or serving people, you would write an S besides that occupation. If your interest in a particular occupation is based mainly on creating and self-expression, you would write an A besides that occupation. Please complete this personality–environment matching exercise before continuing on.

IDENTIFYING SPECIFIC OCCUPATIONS FOR FURTHER RESEARCH

Review both lists of occupations from Step 1 and Step 2 above, and on the blank lines below write any occupations from *either list* that you want to further investigate at this time:

1. _____

2. _____

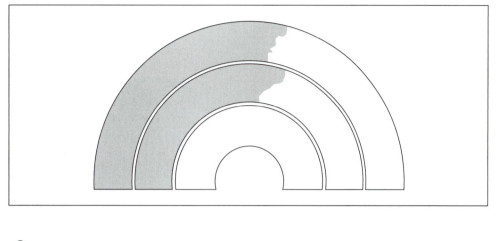

3. _____

4. _____

5. _____

6. _____

7. _____

8. _____

9. _____

10. _____

You now have a safety net—confirmation that the career you are pursuing is right for you. And now you also have a list of other occupations to explore if you discover that your initial career choice is not a good fit after all.

Turn to Appendix 2 on page 93, and follow the directions under "Part IV: Matching." This will provide an important synthesis for the work you have completed, and better prepare you for the next activities in your workbook. Do this now, then continue with this workbook.

You are now ready to continue on to Part V: "Learning More About the Occupation(s) That Match You."

DISCOVERY IS A JOURNEY, NOT A DESTINATION.

PART

V

Spotlight Summary: Researching
Preferred Occupations
Information Resources; ACT
Interactive Web Site; Occupational
Research; Informational
Interviews/Networking

LEARNING MORE ABOUT THE OCCUPATIONS THAT MATCH YOU

But first a little review...

Earlier in this workbook you learned that five ingredients of the career-life strategy formula are (1) self-knowledge, (2) information about the world-of-work, (3) using a reflective decision-making process, (4) understanding the career-life concept, and (5) discovering the best person–environment matches for yourself in your career-life roles.

Also in Part I you learned about some of your self-assessed interests, skills, and work values, and you identified a personal self-knowledge △ code now referred to as your *Holland code.*

In Part III and Part IV, by reviewing how the world-of-work is organized, you were able to identify some specific career clusters, career areas, and occupations that seem to match your Holland code.

Part V will focus on helping you discover specific occupational and labor market information that relates to your preferred occupations.

INFORMATION RESOURCES FOR EXPLORATION

If you are *very focused* at this point and are seriously considering a specific occupation, you might want to quickly review the 16 questions on pages 72–74 now, before trying to answer them. This way, you can decide which information resources might best assist you with your occupational research. For example, if you have access to a computer-assisted career guidance system (CACGS) you can obtain practically all the necessary occupational information in less than an hour and take it home with you on your own personal computer printout. Of course, obtaining the same information from written resources will take more time—perhaps more than one visit to your career center. If you have Internet access, you can obtain most of the information online from home or at the library.

If you are only *fairly decided or uncertain* about which occupation to fully research using the 16 questions, you might want to review your "Specific Occupations for Further Research" on pages 64–65 and begin some preliminary exploration of several of the occupations you listed. As you learn more about these occupations, you will immediately know whether or not to keep focusing on them. Let your feelings and intuition guide you in this process, but make sure you learn enough about each occupation before eliminating it.

There are several sources of information you can use to gather information about the occupations that you think would be a good fit with your Holland code.

Occupational Outlook Handbook

One very good resource is the *Occupational Outlook Handbook* (OOH) published by the U.S. Department of Labor. It is available in most libraries, or online at the Web site of the Bureau of Labor Statistics (www.bls.gov/oco/). It has lots of labor market and salary information, as well as preparation and training information. The online version complements your activities in this workbook. You can click on the A–Z Index at the top of the home page for access to several hundred occupations that will cover many of the actual choices you have narrowed down. Click on your selected occupation for the following information:

- Nature of the work
- Working conditions
- Training, other qualifications, and advancement
- Employment
- Job outlook
- Earnings
- Related occupations
- Sources of additional information including Web sites and instant links

Career Kokua

Another resource is one of the many CACGSs located in most career centers. Many such systems are located in college career centers. Many colleges, even entire states, have agreements with the companies who develop and market these systems to provide access to users from their homes via the Internet. Some popular CACGSs are DISCOVER, SIGI, CHOICES, COIN, and Career Kokua.

Career Kokua (*kokua* is the Hawaiian word for "help") is a system I helped to develop in the late 1970s and is now Internet-based and serves thousands of users throughout the islands of Hawaii. It offers many useful self-assessment and occupational exploration tools, including information about education and training opportunities, financial aid, and job strategies. It also offers excellent links for users planning career choices that involve Hawaii or the mainland. There is even a new job-seekers link called HireNet Hawaii (http://hawaii.gov/labor) for anyone seeking to work in paradise! Check it out if you like gentle trade winds, lots of sunshine, surf, and shaved ice! The Career Kokua site (www.careerkokua.org/) is colorful, easy to navigate, and always filled with helpful career tips for students, parents, and career services providers.

Very recently, the state of Hawaii has arranged for all Hawaii residents to have free access to all the Career Kokua files via the Internet to encourage career exploration and planning statewide. Phyllis Dayao, director of Career Kokua, invites you to visit and browse the site on behalf of the state of Hawaii. *Aloha and mahalo nui loa Hawaii!* ("Warm greetings and thank you very much, to the good career providers in Hawaii!") Simply visit the Web site and at the top-left side of the Career Kokua home page, click "Need a login?" (after the Sign In box) and then follow the directions below:

- If you are a Hawaii resident, go to Option 2 (Hawaii resident login), and enter your City/Town and Zip Code and you will immediately enter the system.

- If you are from another state and would like to browse Career Kokua, click on the link below Option 2 to contact Career Kokua. The staff will respond to your inquiry with a user password within 48 hours.

Discover

Another exciting system that I had the pleasure to pilot in Hawaii and have also used in Massachusetts is ACT's DISCOVER system. DISCOVER offers many creative ways to find occupations in addition to the interest, abilities, and work values inventories. These include searching through the DISCOVER occupation files by "Alpha List," by major, by military experience, by characteristics of occupations, by "Hot Occs" (a search of occupations based on highest salary, fastest growing, or largest number of new openings), and by using the ACT World-of-Work Map.

DISCOVER has a number of other search strategies that provide a rich environment for career exploration. It is loaded with excellent self-assessment tools and offers complete, current databases of occupations, college majors, schools, training institutions, military options, and links to financial aid and scholarships. Users can also learn how to develop effective job-seeking skills through assistance with résumés, cover letters, job applications, and interviewing skills.

DISCOVER has many excellent Internet links. One enjoyable ACT link that fits perfectly with your workbook activities is located at www.actstudent.org/wwm/plan_world.html. This link provides an interactive World-of-Work Map and allows you to click on any part of the map to search for information. You can click on the work tasks (People, Data, Things, Ideas, or a combination of these) around the map's perimeter to obtain a brief summary of the characteristics of people who like working at those tasks. You can also click on any of the career areas inside the map to obtain a list of occupations in your selected area, as well as current and accurate information about work tasks, salary, size and growth of the occupation, entry requirements, related occupations, related job training, courses, and majors that best prepare you for that occupation. You will enjoy this easy and fun interactive link, and it will assist you with your workbook activities.

JA Worldwide

An interactive site that is very useful for high school juniors, seniors, and college freshmen is JA Worldwide (www.ja.org). Click on the Student Center and then the "Find a Career" link, and you'll reach the JA Career Center. There, the world-of-work is classified into 16 career clusters. Each JA career cluster leads you to specific industry information, pathways (groupings of related occupations within a main career cluster), and finally specific occupations with many useful links to free career exploration and job search resources.

National Career Development Association

Another excellent resource packed with information is the National Career Development Association (NCDA) Web site at www.ncda.org, where you can click on the Resources heading on the top of the home page to locate Internet sites for career planning. From here you can link to some of the best Web sites for adult career deciders—ranging from occupational information and job banks to salary information and educational information.

Your Own State's Career Information System

If you prefer to access career information at a Web site in your own state, visit the Association of Computer-Based Systems for Career Information (ACSCI) at www.acsci. org and click on Membership Information at the top of the home page to reach a colorful map of the United States. Locate your state and click on it to access your local career information system. There you will find local occupational and labor market information plus many useful resources and tips to assist you with career exploration and planning.

Other Useful Internet Sites

There are many other Internet sites that provide important and useful information about labor market trends, training programs, resources and services for special needs populations, and even addresses of local service providers. Some of these are described below.

> **www.idealist.org** Some people want to work for a worthy cause. They find this to be more rewarding than choosing a job based solely on income. Idealist.org is an online resource that helps you discover job openings, internship postings, and nonprofit career fairs. It has a Career Center that provides job seekers with tips and resources regarding opportunities, both domestically and abroad.

> **www.ed.gov/students** Learning is a lifelong process. It is important to discover resources that will support your student role—whether you continue your education and training right after high school, or return to college later (for example, after raising a family) to update your skills and prepare yourself for reentering the labor market. This Web site of the U.S. Department of Education provides information and resources for aspiring students on a variety of topics—including choosing and paying for career or technical training; planning for, enrolling in, and paying for college; and returning to school.

> **www.careeronestop.org** Many excellent links, including job banks, are available at the CareerOneStop site. One-Stop Career Centers are located throughout

many communities nationally and provide job seekers with information about training, labor market trends, job search strategies, and more.

www.disabilityinfo.gov Reentry strategies for job seekers with disabilities can be obtained at the DisabilityInfo.gov site. It includes links to school-to-work options, information for veterans and military communities, and vocational rehabilitation resources.

www.aarp.org/careers Job seekers who have significant experience in the world-of-work might encounter some degree of age bias—and might need to stress their enthusiasm, up-to-date skills, and ability to learn new tasks quickly rather than the many jobs described on their résumés outlining a lengthy work history. Information and resources for workers aged 50 and older are available at this AARP site.

www.doleta.gov/jobseekers/laidoff_workers.cfm This Department of Labor site is for people who have experienced involuntary layoffs. Laid-off workers should try to seek another job as soon as possible, to avoid large gaps in employment. This site provides employment and training resources for workers who might need assistance dealing with their situation.

www.hirenetwork.org Ex-offenders are not much different from other job seekers, but they do have some special concerns. Their best steps are probably to seek short-term employment to get back into the rhythm of working, or to obtain immediate education and training, rather than trying to pursue long-term career goals. The National H.I.R.E. Network site provides many resources including state-specific information about the rules and procedures ex-offenders are required to follow when job seeking.

As you can see, there are many computerized and non-computerized resources. Your counselor will be able to direct you to the best resources available at your college or career center or from your home computer.

> The main task at this point in your workbook is to narrow down your alternatives to two or three specific occupations that you are inclined to fully research. When you have completed this selection process, write two or three of your preferred occupations on the blank lines below. Do this now, and then continue on to the exercise, "Occupational Research."

My Occupations for Further Research

1. _____
2. _____
3. _____

OCCUPATIONAL RESEARCH

As you begin to research the occupation(s) that you think will be a good match to your Holland code, here are 16 questions you should ask yourself. (Refer to pages 64–65 as needed to assist you with your research.)

1. Select *one* occupation in, or closely related to, a World-of-Work Map career area that interests you and write its name on the space below.

   _____

2. Review Part III of this workbook and in the spaces provided below write the requested information that relates to your selected occupation.

   a. Career area letter (A–Z) and title: _____

   b. Career cluster name (there are only six): _____

   c. World-of-Work Map region (list specific region number 1–12): _____

   d. World-of-Work Map work task (indicate major emphasis on People, Data, Things, or Ideas): _____

   e. The main Holland code letter (RIASEC) located around the perimeter of the World-of-Work Map on page 52: _____

3. Name three occupations closely related to your selected occupation that might also be of interest to you and could be *bridge* occupations:

   a. _____

   b. _____

   c. _____

4. INTERESTS: List three specific duties and/or responsibilities of the occupation that are of special interest to you. (Review page 11 for examples of your interests.)

   a. _____

   b. _____

   c. _____

5. SKILLS: In the left-hand column below, list three of your top aptitudes or skills that might make this occupation a good choice for you. In the right-hand column, list three skills you *need*. (Review page 14 for examples of your skills.)

   Skills I Have   **Skills I Need**

   a. _____   a. _____

   b. _____   b. _____

   c. _____   c. _____

6. VALUES: Identify three of your work values or things that are very important to you, and briefly explain how this occupation might allow you to express your three values. (Review page 17 for examples of your work values.)

   a. _____

   is an important work value to me, and this occupation will provide me the opportunity to express this value because _____

   _____

b. _____

is an important work value to me, and this occupation will provide me the opportunity to express this value because _____

_____

_____

c. _____

is an important work value to me, and this occupation will provide me the opportunity to express this value because

_____

_____

7. Briefly describe the typical work setting of this occupation.

_____

_____

_____

8. Briefly explain the education or special training necessary for entry into and advancement within the occupation.

_____

_____

9. What other training not offered at your college would be helpful? (Specify type of training and provide reasons.)

_____

_____

_____

10. List three schools or places for further training where preparation for this particular occupation is offered.

School   **Location**

a. _____

b. _____

c. _____

11. What is the beginning salary range? $_____ to $_____
per hour/week/month/year (circle one)

12. What the salary range of experienced employees? $_____ to $_____
per hour/week/month/year (circle one)

13. Describe the employment outlook for this occupation and the major reason(s) for this outlook.

_____

_____

_____

14. List two addresses (including contact persons if possible) where you can obtain further information about this occupation. (Your career center might have a community resource file to help you research this question.)

a. Company/Agency: _____

    Address: _____

    E-mail:_____ Phone: _____ Contact: _____

b. Company/Agency: _____

    E-mail:_____ Phone: _____ Contact: _____

15. List one or two bridge jobs that would allow you to gain important experience and on-the-job training, to prepare you to eventually obtain your preferred occupation.

    a. _____

    b. _____

16. If you were unable, for some reason, to obtain *paid* employment in this occupation, yet wanted to have an outlet for your interests and work values similar to those associated with this occupation in some of your other career-life rainbow roles, briefly describe the leisure (hobby) or citizen (volunteer) activities that you might consider.

Leisure Role: _____

_____

Citizen Role: _____

_____

By researching the answers to the preceding 16 questions, you have provided yourself with sufficient information to further narrow down alternatives and evaluate your options. More research might be needed, and discussing some of your findings with your counselor or instructor might be helpful.

> *You may now continue on to the next exercise, "The Informational Interview."*

THE INFORMATIONAL INTERVIEW

One other way of researching your options is actually speaking to someone who works in the field you are investigating. The following exercise will assist you in organizing and implementing a series of informational interviews related to your tentative occupational choices.

The informational interview is a powerful means of gathering information and simultaneously making some important community contacts—including possibly even obtaining a job offer!

> *If you do not wish to do the following optional exercise at this time, you may move ahead to Part VI.*

PYRAMIDING FOR SUCCESS

This exercise is optional. It is mainly intended for people interested in learning more about a particular field or specific type of work, or people enrolled (or soon to be) in cooperative education, job shadowing, or other related programs that encourage actual contact with employers for the purpose of learning more about a selected occupation. If your college is presently (or soon to be) working with you in actual job placement activities, you might find this exercise highly beneficial.

The key to this exercise is always to get two names from each person you contact. One leads to two, two to four, four to eight. It's that simple and very powerful!

Objectives of the Informational Interview

Your objective in an informational interview is to meet and develop a network of knowledgeable and well-connected people who work in employment settings you are considering. These people will be in a position to refer you to their personal contacts—and might even be in a position to hire you in the future.

Your objective is *not* to speak to people in Human Resources or whatever department is usually responsible for the hiring process. You should *not* present yourself as looking for employment. If you do present yourself this way, you might find yourself talking to a receptionist and being handed application forms to fill out or general information forms about the company or agency. You should clearly indicate that you are doing an *informational interview*—that is, researching specific information about an occupation, as opposed to looking for immediate employment. (The traditional job interview process is discussed in Appendix 3, which includes cover letters and résumés.)

You should present yourself as an interested and motivated person wanting to meet with a vice president, president, general manager, or perhaps a project director in order to do a brief informational interview about the company or agency, its products and services, and its direction. These are the key people who can best provide you with the information you want and who will most likely enjoy helping you with your "research project." You might want to use some modification of the following approach:

> "Hello. My name is . . . and I would very much appreciate some assistance for this research project I am doing on [your selected occupation or field]. I have done some preliminary research on your company. I have brief list of questions and will need about 20 to 25 minutes if that is possible. I would appreciate your help."

Of course, even though you are not officially job hunting, these same people are the individuals who would be in a position to offer you a job—if one were to become available. Keep this in mind! People are *always* looking for good talent!

Even though you are not going for a job interview, dress and act in an appropriate manner. You will be giving impressions to the people meeting you, and first impressions are often lasting impressions.

How to Use the Interview to Develop Your Personal Pyramid Network of Employer Contacts

So now you have your objectives in mind, and maybe even a specific company or agency that you want to visit for your informational interview. How do you use the interview to develop your network of contacts? There are four steps, as follows:

STEP 1. Begin the process by researching the occupation and employment setting you have selected. For example, if you are planning an informational interview related to accounting, you should become familiar not only with the occupation of accounting in general, but also with ABC Accounting firm, the employment setting where you plan your first informational interview.

Prepare five questions related to the occupation you are researching, including one or two that relate to the specific employment setting you are visiting. A list of suggested informational interview questions appears on pages 77–78. As recommended on that list, make sure your last question is: "Would you please provide me with the names and phone numbers of two other colleagues you personally know who hold company positions similar to your own and who would be willing to share some time with me for a informational interview?"

STEP 2. Select a company for your initial interview. Contact the company and inform the receptionist that you are doing an informational interview as a special project and would very much appreciate speaking to the vice president, general manager, or other appropriate person. (It is best to have an actual name here to alert the receptionist that you have some *knowledge of the person you are intending to interview and that person's company position*.)

Also inform the receptionist that the interview will take only about 20 to 25 minutes. Make sure you keep it under 25 minutes, unless the person you are interviewing wants to spend more time speaking with you. *Be on time*—preferably arriving 10 minutes before your scheduled appointment. Bring a cup of coffee and/or small box of donuts for the receptionist.

STEP 3. After a firm handshake (this should be done before and after each interview and is appropriate for both women and men) and a sincere verbal acknowledgement of your appreciation for the time and dialogue that person is sharing with you, begin your informational interview. Show enthusiasm for your future involvement in the field. Take notes, and be an attentive listener. You might hear some very wise words of advice during this interview. After the interview, promptly mail a brief handwritten thank-you note—within 48 hours. Make sure you include your home address, and write the letter neatly with your best cursive handwriting. If you have sufficient funds to purchase some inexpensive personalized stationery, this is a convenient way to pass on your address and home telephone.

STEP 4. Write the date of contact, name, position, company name and address, phone number, e-mail address, and Web site URL of your first contact person at the top center area of a blank piece of paper. Below that (in pencil, because you might not actually reach these people) add the names and phone numbers of the two persons whose names you received from your first source.

Personal Pyramid Network

Level 1

Date _____

Name _____

Position _____

Company _____

Address _____

_____

Phone _____

E-mail _____; Web site _____

Level 2

Date _____   Date _____

Name _____   Name _____

Position _____   Position _____

Company _____   Company _____

Address _____   Address _____

_____   _____

Phone _____   Phone _____

E-mail _____; Web site _____   E-mail _____; Web site _____

Level 3

Date _____   Date _____   Date _____   Date _____

Repeat these steps with each person you visit, to develop the next level of your personal pyramid network. Ideally, you should continue the process to include a minimum of seven interviews. You will have then developed three levels at this stage. (See the Personal Pyramid Network diagram above.)

You might want to continue to build on your personal pyramid, but seven informational interviews (three levels) should provide you with sufficient information to help you learn a great deal about the specific occupation. You will also have the names and addresses of seven key individuals you have personally met—individuals who might be in a position to hire you in the future. Keep this information in a file for future use. Some persons who have used this process have received actual job offers at Level 2 or 3.

Suggested Informational Interview Questions

1. Please describe what you find to be a typical workday or workweek, including routine work flow and major work tasks that need to be accomplished.

2. Please share what you find to be the main positive aspects of your job and the main negative aspects as well, if there are any.

3. Please share some of your own career experiences—how and why you first became involved in your present position, where you were prior to your present position, and in general how your career has developed over the years, including what motivated you to consider your first career choice.

4. If you had a crystal ball, what predictions would you make about the future of this occupation (company), not only in terms of employment demand, but also involvement with new technologies, new target groups, and perhaps new products?

5. Would you please provide me with the names and phone numbers of two other colleagues you personally know who hold company positions similar to your own and who would be willing to share some time with me for a informational interview?

You may now continue on to Part VI: "Your Future Career-Life Situation."

PART VI

Spotlight Summary: Preparing for Your Future; Relevance of Your College Education; Having the Right Attitude; "The Golden Coconut"

YOUR FUTURE CAREER-LIFE SITUATION

Self-Knowledge and the Learning Process

Your College Education and Your Career-Life Future

Some people are more certain of their career and life goals than others, and there are many different and good reasons for attending college or seeking further training or education after high school. Research clearly indicates that college graduates earn higher salaries and experience lower unemployment rates.

Arriving at college totally undecided about your future is common, but *leaving* college the same way can cause great angst, including having to make those loan payments for many years.

You can apply the self-knowledge gained from this workbook to formal and informal learning situations throughout your life. For example, taking college courses does more than accumulate credits toward your degree. You are learning content information and subject matter, how to evaluate and appreciate new ideas, and how to be a critical thinker. You can use your college courses to constantly *learn about yourself*—your aptitudes and abilities, your interests and values, and what in life is important to you.

Several of the reasons many people attend college are to prepare for satisfying careers, to take courses that will improve on-the-job performance, or simply to enjoy courses for the sake of enrichment.

If you already have a tentative career in mind or are presently employed, you can take advantage of the information and skill-building opportunities that college courses can provide. In this framework, your courses and your entire education are an important part of your training and preparation for the world-of-work.

However, even if you are uncertain about your goals, college major, or specific career area, your courses can still provide important information and skill-building opportunities. Simply writing a term paper, taking part in a class discussion, or making an individual or group presentation can contribute to your learning, your improved self-concept, and your total educational experience.

There is much to learn about yourself when you take a college course. If you enjoy the course and find it easy, ask yourself why. If the course seems difficult, try to understand why you are having problems. Even if the course seems boring, you might discover some good reasons, other than the instructor, to explain why you don't find the subject matter stimulating. For example, if you're taking math or chemistry and do not enjoy the course at all, after some reflection you might discover that you don't enjoy situations requiring structure and specific details. This is important self-knowledge to understand and remember in your career-life planning, especially if this dislike for structure and details is recurring throughout your life.

Begin to monitor yourself while you are taking courses. Learn to be a reflective thinker. Concentrate on the course content, and also learn to understand your feelings about the course and your reasons for these feelings. You can learn more about yourself and your feelings when you ask yourself four basic words: "What is there about . . . ?" What is there about enjoying (or not enjoying) a particular course? What is there about doing well (or not doing well) in a particular course? As you better understand your feelings, you will also learn more about the richness of the course content, and the relationship between that content and you as a unique individual and a unique learner.

You will discover that learning can be enjoyable and rewarding in a very personal way—and this experience can move your life in some powerful directions because learning is a lifelong process.

Developing the Right Attitude

Hopefully you now have a clearer understanding of yourself, the world-of-work, and even specific occupations in the world-of-work that interest to you. Making career-life decisions is sometimes a slow process. This workbook might have helped you with your present situation, but you will be making career-life decisions for a long time to come. Many of the ideas in this workbook can be applied to those future decisions as well.

Having the right attitude about how to deal with your career-life decisions is important. Take your time and explore your options carefully. It's possible to become impatient, especially if others around you are too forceful with their opinions about what you should be doing with your future. They probably mean well, but remember that the final word rests within *you*. You really do create your own destiny—and wanting to change your present situation is the first step to creating your future direction.

Many factors will influence your future, but *you* have the most to do with how, where, and when your future actually develops and unfolds. *Knowing what's most important to you* is the first step in achieving something or going somewhere in your life journey. Knowing what you *need*—your values—is the power behind that first step.

The following exercise will help you identify what you need right now—and how and where to take that first step.

THE GOLDEN COCONUT R

This 15-minute exercise deals with your future and will be more effective and enjoyable if completed when you are alone and quiet.

Imagine yourself on the beautiful Hawaiian island of Kauai, known as the Garden Isle, where there are lush green forests that landscape the rolling hills and magnificent mountain cliffs called *Na Pali*. In one quiet, secluded little valley protected by tall mountains on two sides and the blue-green ocean on the other, there is a narrow stretch of beach. The beach sand is as soft as powder and as golden as the sun that reflects on the white caps of the powerful surf splashing down with a thunderous roar, leaving a continuous golden mist in the entire area.

Nearby is a clump of Royal Hawaiian palm trees known for their tall, very straight shape. In the center of these Royal palms is one unique coconut tree that contains special Golden Coconuts. These coconuts grow very slowly over the years, and every so often, one will be loosened by the trade winds and fall onto the soft sand below.

You have heard of an ancient legend that says someone who discovers one of these Golden Coconuts can find the end of the rainbow and have three wishes granted, but only after opening the Golden Coconut and drinking its sweet coconut milk.

You have been hiking alone all morning near this secluded area of Kauai, and—quite by accident—you find a narrow pass between the two mountains, leading to the remote beach. As you walk onto the soft, warm sand, suddenly you spot the legendary coconut tree. As you look beneath the tree, you are amazed to find a round Golden Coconut that has recently been loosened by the trade winds.

Sitting down on the sand, you open the Golden Coconut and, raising it to your dry lips, you sip the sweet, warm milk.

As you lie back on the sand, a full, beautiful, colorful rainbow immediately appears . . .

STEP 1. Review your present career-life rainbow (page 41 in Part II) to briefly reflect where you are right now in your life journey. Carefully examine each role by checking your satisfaction ratings (see "Evaluating My Present Career-Life Roles" on page 41). Think about what you *still need to be doing* in each role to *significantly improve it and make it more fulfilling.* Identify one or two specific actions that you believe would *improve* the time and energy you need to be spending in each of your career-life rainbow roles to make a difference. Write these actions in the appropriate spaces below. If you *will not* be playing a specific role, do not address that role now. You might want to revisit this activity in a few months or a year to review your reflections and make any appropriate adjustments.

Take at least several minutes to do Step 1. You might close your eyes to be more in touch with your intuition and real feelings. Do Step 1 now before continuing on.

Child (daughter/son). The time and energy you need to spend in your relationship to your parents or guardians:

1. _____

2. _____

Student. The time and energy you need to spend in education or training:

1. _____

2. _____

Worker. The time and energy you need to spend in work for pay:

1. _____

2. _____

Spouse/Friendship. The time and energy you need to spend in your relationship with your husband, wife, or close friends:

1. _____

2. _____

Homemaker. The time and energy you need to spend taking responsibility for home maintenance and management:

1. _____

2. _____

Parent. The time and energy you need to spend nurturing your relationship with your children:

1. _____

2. _____

Leisurite. The time and energy you need to spend enjoying leisure, spare-time activities, and hobbies:

1. _____

2. _____

Citizen. The time and energy you need to spend volunteering in civic, church, political, or community activities:

1. _____

2. _____

Annuitant. The time and energy you need to spend preparing for the role that replaces Worker—that is, the time in life when you receive Social Security, a pension, or other types of retirement income:

1. _____

2. _____

STEP 2. You have successfully reviewed your present career-life situation. You have identified various actions that you believe will improve the quality of time and energy across several of your career-life rainbow roles. Good job. Now you have the opportunity to review your ideas and select *the three most important actions that you need to accomplish first* because you believe these three will *immediately improve your situation.*

Remember, the Golden Coconut grants you only *three* wishes, and you need to focus and believe that these wishes will come true. Review what you have written in Step 1 indicating the important changes you believe are necessary for improving your career-life situation. Select three actions that are the *most important* for you at this time because of the *immediate* effect they will have on your life journey, and circle them. You can select two different wishes that deal with the same career-life role and a third wish from a different role, or you can select three separate wishes, each from a different role. You are free to wish whatever is your heart's desire in any of the career-life rainbow bands—but you should circle three wishes. Circle your three wishes now before continuing on.

Now carefully review your three circled wishes and rank them in order of which one you want to happen first, then second, and finally third. On the blank lines below—inside the large self-knowledge pyramid icon that is your source of inspiration and power—write down your three wishes, making sure to indicate their order of importance. These three wishes can make a great difference in your life! Do this now before continuing on.

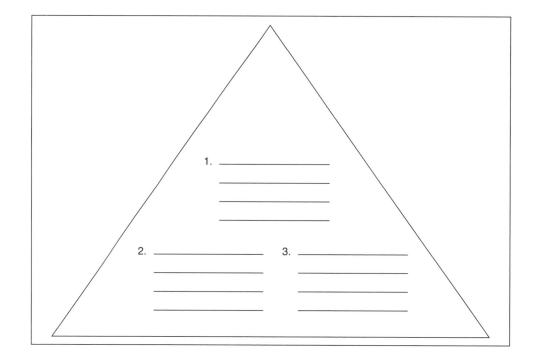

1. _____
   _____
   _____
   _____

2. _____   3. _____
   _____   _____
   _____   _____
   _____   _____

What's to come is what's in your heart and mind—but only the power of believing, followed by appropriate action, can bring results and fulfillment to your future.

Start believing in yourself right now, and know what you need and want out of life. Read the three wishes you listed in the self-knowledge pyramid icon and begin to focus on what needs to be done to get your life moving.

> **"A man who becomes conscious of the responsibility he bears toward a human being who affectionately waits for him, or to an unfinished work, will never be able to throw away his life. He knows the 'why' for his existence, and will be able to bear almost any 'how.'"**
>
> —VIKTOR FRANKL

Continue on to Part VII to develop your individual action plan for selecting and implementing Your Best Next Step.

PART VII

Spotlight Summary: Your Next Steps; Identifying Objectives in All Your Career-Life Roles; Selecting and Implementing Your Best Next Step

CREATING YOUR RAINBOW

Well, this is it! You have reached the final section of *Creating Careers with Confidence*. You might be on the cutting edge of an important career-life decision! If making such decisions has always been easy for you, then you're probably not very excited at this time. Your work thus far might simply have confirmed your original career-life choice, and so you might be relieved about being on the right track, but perhaps not really "excited."

However, if you've had some difficulty making such decisions—and most of us do—then the effort you have put into this workbook should be paying off just about now. You have a right to be feeling enlightened, more confident, and somewhat upbeat—perhaps even *excited about your future*. You have a right to be positive and optimistic about yourself and your life journey. Never let anyone take that from you. If you do, you are giving away your power!

You have now successfully learned and used a practical career-life strategy; become aware of your self-assessed skills, interests, and work-related values; evaluated your present career-life situation; researched occupational information that matches your self-knowledge; and identified three career-life actions that you believe will *immediately* improve your career-life situation. You have worked hard at thinking about who you are. Congratulations on your effort!

At this point you might feel the need to more clearly crystallize your thoughts and develop a specific action plan to begin your career-life journey. The final workbook exercise will help you examine some realistic "next step" objectives related to your career-life plans and then help you identify your *best next step*—the one step that will get you moving in the right direction.

This "best next step" needs to be one that:

- Is within your reach

- Moves you in the right direction

- Produces immediate, positive results

You might find it useful to review "The Five-Minute Rainbow Connection" on pages 5–6, the discussion of "My Ideal Career Scenario" on pages 17–19, and Step 2 of "The Golden Coconut" exercise on pages 81–84 to better focus on what kinds of "next steps" are most important to you right now in your life. Do this now before continuing on.

YOUR BEST NEXT STEP

STEP 1. The following are suggested "next step" objectives related to two of Donald super's nine major roles in the career-life rainbow: the student role and the worker role. Review the suggested student-related and worker-related "next step" objectives in the left-hand column below adding some of your own. Then fill in the corresponding blank lines in the right-hand column on that page with specific details that relate to each objective. Your "next step" objectives should be those that make the most sense to you at this time based on all your reflections with this workbook. Be creative, yet wise. Don't underestimate yourself—but try to establish objectives that *need* to be done and *can* be done by *you.*

"NEXT STEP" OBJECTIVES FOR CAREER–LIFE RAINBOW ROLES

Student-Related Next Step Objectives

Specific Details (name of person and office location, title of book or course to be taken, etc.)

A. Courses I could take to further explore my interests or develop specific skills

A. _____ _____

B. Instructors/counselors or people in the community I could meet who might help me clarify my thoughts or provide information

B. _____ _____

C. Places I could visit that might provide me with information or assistance (career center, learning assistance center, library, etc.)

C. _____ _____

D. Books, articles, films, or Internet resources I could use for further exploration and planning

D. _____ _____

List any other "next step" objectives and related specific details:

E. _____ _____

E. _____ _____

F. _____ _____

F. _____ _____

Worker-Related Next Step Objectives

Specific Details (name of person and office location, etc.)

A. Part-time jobs, cooperative education internships, or job shadowing experiences I might enjoy

A. _____ _____

B. Contact person(s) who can provide me with the necessary information I will need

B. _____

C. Preparation required for obtaining a job or initiating a job shadowing experience (developing my résumé, researching a company, conducting more informational interviews, etc.)

C. _____ _____

*List any other "next step" objectives and
related specific details:*

D. _____ D. _____

_____ _____

E. _____ E. _____

_____ _____

If you have some other "next step" objectives that relate to any of the remaining seven major career/life rainbow roles, list these objectives and corresponding details on the appropriate spaces provided below.

**Son/Daughter-Related
Next Step Objectives**

Specific Details

A. _____ A. _____

_____ _____

B. _____ B. _____

_____ _____

C. _____ C. _____

_____ _____

**Spouse/Friendship-Related
Next Step Objectives**

Specific Details

A. _____ A. _____

_____ _____

B. _____ B. _____

_____ _____

C. _____ C. _____

_____ _____

**Homemaker-Related
Next Step Objectives**

Specific Details

A. _____ A. _____

_____ _____

B. _____ B. _____

_____ _____

C. _____ C. _____

_____ _____

**Parent-Related
Next Step Objectives**

Specific Details

A. _____ A. _____

_____ _____

B. _____   B. _____

_____   _____

C. _____   C. _____

_____   _____

Leisurite-Related
Next Step Objectives   **Specific Details**

A. _____   A. _____

_____   _____

B. _____   B. _____

_____   _____

C. _____   C. _____

_____   _____

Citizen-Related
Next Step Objectives   **Specific Details**

A. _____   A. _____

_____   _____

B. _____   B. _____

_____   _____

C. _____   C. _____

_____   _____

Annuitant-Related
Next Step Objectives   **Specific Details**

A. _____   A. _____

_____   _____

B. _____   B. _____

_____   _____

C. _____   C. _____

_____   _____

STEP 2. Now that you have identified specific "next step" objectives that are relevant to your career-life exploration and planning, carefully review all of those objectives and corresponding specific details. Circle the *one* objective that you feel is your *best* next step, and circle the specific details you indicated that need to be done to accomplish that objective.

Reread the objectives and specific details for your best "next step"—and be firmly resolved to do what you have written down. On the following blank lines, write down the objectives and specific details of your best next step and assign it to yourself as a task. Also give yourself a realistic date for completing each part of this task.

I'm going to assign myself the task of... (be specific):   Completion date:_____

_____

_____

_____

_____

_____

_____

_____

_____

_____

_____

_____

_____

_____

_____

_____

_____

_____

_____

_____

_____

_____

> **The artist is nothing without the gift, but the gift is nothing without work.**
> –ÉMILE ZOLA

It is important to plan ahead and take charge of your life—but also recognize that good *and* bad luck showers upon everyone. Life is filled with luck—be aware of its presence when it affects you. You can often organize it and maximize your benefits!

Also—just like the angel in "The Choice" at the beginning of this workbook—remember that you have a responsibility to share yourself with creation and contribute something positive to our world and universe. You might choose to do this by using any of the career-life rainbow roles: You might lead a nation, sing a song, plant a tree, or teach a child. It doesn't matter what you choose to do as long as what you do is truly *you*.

Always be willing to know yourself, to dare to dream, and to make your dreams become reality. Draw inspiration from the base of your rainbow—your self-knowledge △, especially your values, the cornerstone of your "pyramid for success."

Never be afraid or ashamed to ask another person for a helping hand or perhaps a few words to guide you. We all need mentors!

Consider that if you don't know where you're going in life, you'll probably end up someplace else!

Good luck with all of your career-life experiences—and whenever you feel the need to talk and share, your counselor or instructor wants to listen.

Finally, always remember . . .

Rainbows don't just happen—they are created!

APPENDIX 1
CAREER-LIFE THEMES

MY MAIN SUMMARY REFLECTION IN ONE TO THREE WORDS

Review your response to "My Main Summary Reflection in One to Three Words" on page xxix in the Introduction to this workbook and write your one to three words on the line below. Return to your workbook.

_____

MY MAIN SUMMARY THEMES: #1, #2, AND #4

Review your responses to "My Career-Life Themes: The Banyan Tree Exercises" (#1: The Five-Minute Rainbow Connection, #2: My Interests, and #4: My Values) on pages 25–27 in Part I, and write your main one or two emerging summary themes on the lines below.

_____

_____

EVALUATING MY PRESENT CAREER-LIFE ROLES

Activity A

Review each role you rated as FS or US/SF in "Evaluating My Present Career-Life Roles" on page 40 in Part II, and on the lines below write the main reason you rated each of these as FS or US/SF. Note any recurring themes that need further examination.

Child (daughter/son): The time and energy spent in your relationship to your parents or guardians.

_____

Student: The time and energy spent in education or training.

_____

Worker: The time and energy spent working for pay.

_____

Spouse/Friendship: The time and energy spent in your relationship with your husband, wife, or close friends.

_____

Homemaker: The time and energy spent in taking responsibility for home maintenance and management.

_____

Parent: The time and energy spent in your relationship with your children.

_____

Leisurite: The time and energy spent in leisure or spare-time activities.

_____

Citizen: The time and energy spent in civic, church, political, or community activities.

_____

Annuitant: The time and energy spent preparing for the role that replaces Worker—that is, the time in life when you will receive Social Security, a pension, or other types of retirement income.

_____

Activity B

Now review the "ABC's for a Vibrant and Successful Rainbow" on page 42 in Part II, and on the lines below write any insights you have regarding how best to deal with the difficulties you are experiencing in the roles you rated as FS or US/SF.

Child (daughter/son): The time and energy spent in your relationship to your parents or guardians.

_____

Student: The time and energy spent in education or training.

_____

Worker: The time and energy spent working for pay.

_____

Spouse/Friendship: The time and energy spent in your relationship with your husband, wife, or close friends.

_____

Homemaker: The time and energy spent in taking responsibility for home maintenance and management.

_____

Parent: The time and energy spent in your relationship with your children.

_____

Leisurite: The time and energy spent in leisure or spare-time activities.

_____

Citizen: The time and energy spent in civic, church, political, or community activities.

_____

Annuitant: The time and energy spent preparing for the role that replaces Worker—that is, the time in life when you will receive Social Security, a pension, or other types of retirement income.

_____

APPENDIX 2
IDEAL CAREER SCENARIO

MY IDEAL CAREER SCENARIO #1—DRAFT 1

Review what you have written as your top two or three Holland RIASEC codes under "My Environment Type" on page 45 in Part II, and write the letters in the boxes below.

□ □ □

Next review your summary description under "My Environment Type" on page 45. Use that initial description of your preferred environment type to develop your first draft of *My Ideal Career Scenario* below. Keep in mind that this is a first draft, and does *not* have to be complete. It is better simply to build on a few insights gathered from your workbook activities and personal intuition. Don't try and make this draft perfect. Reflect on this summary description because it is based on the excellent work you have already completed in your workbook.

_____

_____

_____

_____

_____

_____

_____

_____

PART IV: MATCHING

Review your responses to "Using My Holland Code to Match World-of-Work Regions and Career Areas" on page 58 in Part IV, and write the top three ranked letters of your Holland code in the boxes below.

□ □ □

Compare your Holland code in these boxes with your Holland code in the boxes in the previous activity, "My Ideal Career Scenario #1—Draft 1." They should be the same or very similar, with perhaps one of the codes in a different ranked position. If they are the same and the rank order is the same, move ahead to the section marked "Regions and Career Areas" below.

If they are not the same or even similar, recheck your responses to the activities you previously did, noting the appropriate page references, to make sure you copied the code letters accurately. If you did copy them accurately, review the actual activity to see if you responded accurately. If you did respond accurately, ask yourself the following questions, and write your responses on the lines provided:

- Which Holland code letters and rank ordering seem to feel the *most* accurate to me? (Place these code letters in the boxes below.)

■ *Why* does this feel more accurate? (Write your response in the space below the boxes. You might want to speak with your counselor or instructor to gain more clarity.)

☐ ☐ ☐

_____

_____

Now continue to "Regions and Career Areas" below.

REGIONS AND CAREER AREAS

Review your responses to "Using My Holland Code to Match World-of-Work Regions and Career Areas" on page 59 in Part IV, and write the regions and career areas you circled in the spaces at the right of the table below.

Code	Ranking	Regions	Career Areas (A–Z)
R	=	6 and 7	
I	=	7, 8, 9, and 10	
A	=	10 and 11	
S	=	12, 1 and 2	
E	=	2 and 3	
C	=	3, 4 and 5	

Next, review your responses to "Identifying Specific Occupations for Further Research" on pages 64–65 in Part IV, and write the occupations you listed in the spaces below.

1. _____

2. _____

3. _____

4. _____

5. _____

6. _____

7. _____

8. _____

9. _____

10. _____

Finally, review *all* your responses in the Appendix 2 activities. Note the *main* similarities with your Holland code letters, the similarities among matching regions and career areas that share common characteristics, and any similarities among the preferred occupations you have listed. There might be some differences, and that is acceptable. Reflect on the main similarities and your personal observations. Address these two questions:

1. What are the *main* similarities I observe? (Describe those similarities on the lines below, using your knowledge of People, Data, Things, and Ideas and the six Holland code descriptions on pages 13–25 in Part I.)

_____

_____

_____

_____

2. Using the main similarities I observe, how can I now create a more complete draft of *My Ideal Career Scenario* that references my top-ranked Holland codes and my understanding, up to now, about the type of work environment where I would be most fulfilled? (Use the following directions in "My Ideal Career Scenario #1— Draft 2" to assist you with your next draft of *My Ideal Career Scenario.*)

MY IDEAL CAREER SCENARIO #1—DRAFT 2

Write your next draft of *My Ideal Career Scenario*. Call it "Scenario #1, Draft 2." The next version will be "Scenario #1, Draft 3," and so on. (If you decide to create more than one scenario, simply name the second one "My Ideal Career Scenario #2, Draft 1," etc.)

Write your three-letter Holland code here: _____.
(See pages 43–44 in your workbook to better understand your personality type and examples of the work activities and world-of-work options you might enjoy.)

As you create your ideal career, the first paragraph should describe where you would like to live, how long a commute you prefer, whether you prefer to stay in an office setting or be on the road traveling about for your work, and similar specific details.

The last paragraph should reflect how your Holland code can be best reflected through various hobbies and interests, through volunteer work (about two or three hours a month), and throughout your various career-life roles, other than your paid work role. Imagine your lifestyle—the hobbies and interests you want to pursue *outside* work, the volunteer time you would devote to some organization or cause, how you want to spend time in your spouse/partner/friendship/leisure roles, and so forth. Write these thoughts into your ideal career scenario. These first and last paragraphs will usually be the same or very similar throughout the various scenarios and drafts you develop.

For the main part of your ideal career (the middle of your narrative), describe your paid work activities. Use your Holland code as your reference and write several sentences per code letter. List some of the specific activities you would enjoy that match your Holland code. Feel free to use any of the words or phrases that are found in your workbook that describe the Holland code. Refer to pages 58–61 to help you focus on your Holland code and remind yourself where you fit in the World-of-Work Map.

Remember that the Holland code letters RIASEC stand for R = Realistic, I = Investigative, A = Artistic, S = Social, E = Enterprising, and C = Conventional. Indicate every now and then in your ideal career scenario the specific Holland code letters that you believe match your work activities and the expression of your code in all your career-life rainbow roles.

The following questions and suggestions might assist you:

■ Do you want to work mostly with People, Data, Things, Ideas, or some combination of these work tasks? Again, refer to the above suggested page references and review your workbook to help you articulate your preferences. Add specificity when you can. Try to imagine that you have all the talents, degrees, knowledge, confidence, and self-esteem necessary to accomplish your ideal career. Also imagine that *there is a need* for whatever you write about and that *the opportunity is there* for you. Finally, imagine that you have the total support of family, relatives, and friends.

■ How much alone time do you want? How much contact with others do you prefer? Do you want to spend much of your work hours sitting down, or moving about—including perhaps some travel time? When you have contact with others, do you want to manage or coordinate them and their projects, or do you want to work *with* others and participate in a project as a coworker, not as a manager or leader?

■ Remember, this is only a *draft*—a work in progress. Take time to reflect on your ideas as you experience this process. Enjoy this process of creating!

Now write your second draft of *My Ideal Career Scenario* on the lines below.

_____

_____

_____

_____

_____

_____

_____

_____

_____

_____

_____

_____

_____

_____

_____

_____

_____

_____

_____

_____

APPENDIX 3
PERSONAL PORTFOLIO

ACADEMIC ADVISING GUIDE

Most colleges require a core curriculum that relates to your academic degree. If you are taking a liberal arts curriculum, your college catalog will indicate the number of *required courses* such as English, math, and a selection of courses from several areas such as the social sciences, arts and humanities, science, and language arts. Depending on your academic program and field of specialization (such as nursing or accounting), and also depending on the certificate or degree you are seeking (for example, a 30-credit certificate or a two-year or four-year degree), the required course work will vary.

Most programs will allow you to take some *elective courses.* These are courses that do not have to relate to your academic program and career goals. They are simply courses that fulfill your graduation requirement of completing a certain number of credits—and therefore can be any course that interests you.

Courses usually have an *alpha* to indicate the subject matter (for example, ENG = English; HIS = History, and BUS = Business) and a *number* to indicate the level of complexity (for example, 50, or 101, or 312). Courses with an alpha/number below 100 (for example, BUS 50) will usually not transfer from a two-year or community college to an upper division institution or four-year college or university. But these courses might be important to take for other reasons. Discuss this with your college academic advisors or counselors, and consult your college catalog.

Most postsecondary institutions provide *academic advising* that helps you choose the appropriate sequence of courses to best support your academic goals. Many schools also have *career counselors* trained to assist you with discovering career goals. Some schools have staffs that provide a combination of academic and career counseling.

Ultimately, the responsibility rests with *you*—you are the one who needs to make sure you are taking the right sequence of courses that fulfills your degree requirements. You are the person who needs to clarify your career goals, narrow down your suitable options, and take the necessary steps to implement your career exploration and planning process. But remember: You don't have to make these decisions by yourself. When in doubt, don't act—*ask!*

The following activity can help you select your courses. Use it in conjunction with the resources available at your college, and consider it to be an early-planning tool to provide a bird's-eye view of the type of academic advising assistance you need to obtain from your college staff.

Choosing Your College Courses

Fill in the appropriate spaces below. It is important to reflect on your *reasons* for each course and write those reasons in the spaces provided. Share this with your academic advisor or career counselor to obtain the most accurate academic advising information at your college.

Review your responses to "Occupational Research" on pages 72–74 in Part V—especially items 1, 3, 4, 5, 8, 9, and 10—to prepare you for responding to this activity.

1. INTERESTS: Courses provide an excellent means of determining your degree of interest and motivation to eventually declare a major. Reflect on the types of courses that will help you further explore your interests. List them below.

Courses I Will Enjoy That
Relate to My Career Goals   Reasons

1. _____   1. _____
2. _____   2. _____
3. _____   3. _____
4. _____   4. _____
5. _____   5. _____

Notes: _____
_____

2. GOALS: Courses provide an excellent means of learning more about a particular field and exploring related topics. Reflect on the types of courses that will help you further explore your career goals. List them below.

Courses That Will Help Me
Explore My Career Goals   Reasons

1. _____   1. _____
2. _____   2. _____
3. _____   3. _____
4. _____   4. _____
5. _____   5. _____

Notes: _____
_____

3. SKILLS: Courses provide an excellent means of learning new knowledge and acquiring new skills, including testing your abilities to do specific course work. Reflect on the types of courses that will help you explore your abilities and acquire important skills/training for your career goals. List them below.

Courses That Will Provide Me
with Skills/Training and Prepare
Me for My Career Goals   Reasons

1. _____   1. _____
2. _____   2. _____
3. _____   3. _____
4. _____   4. _____
5. _____   5. _____

Notes: _____
_____

4. KNOWLEDGE: Courses provide an excellent means of gaining new perspectives and knowledge about yourself and how others think and behave. Reflect on the types of courses that will help you learn more about yourself, how others think and

behave, and provide you with a general education and preparation for your life and the various life roles you will be playing. List them below.

Courses I Believe Are Important for My General Education and Preparation for My Life

Reasons

1. _____   1. _____
2. _____   2. _____
3. _____   3. _____
4. _____   4. _____
5. _____   5. _____

Notes: _____
_____

5. ENJOYMENT: Courses provide an excellent means of learning more about a topic or field of interest unrelated to your career goals—just because you enjoy that particular topic. Reflect on the types of courses you would truly enjoy just for the fun of taking them. List them below.

Courses I Will Enjoy That Might Not Relate to My Career Goals

Reasons

1. _____   1. _____
2. _____   2. _____
3. _____   3. _____
4. _____   4. _____
5. _____   5. _____

Notes: _____
_____

COVER LETTERS, RÉSUMÉS, AND INTERVIEWS

Cover letters, résumés, and job interviews are important topics, and there are many books and Internet sites that focus on these topics. To make it simple, but hopefully *not* to oversimplify, the following guidelines should provide a good basis for developing your cover letter and résumé, as well as preparing for your job interview. You should also look for books and resources that more comprehensively deal with these topics, and seek assistance from your career counselor as needed.

In a nutshell, your cover letter should *catch the eyes* of the intended reader and influence that person to read your résumé. A résumé is your personal passkey that *opens the door* for your job interview. The interview is an opportunity to *tell your story*. The more effective your cover letter and résumé, the better is your opportunity to tell your story and be discovered!

Your Cover Letter

Your cover letter should be a one-page statement that personally and professionally expresses your interest in the position, articulates a brief summary of your qualifications, and very sincerely and skillfully advertises your unique contributions so that the reader *wants* to learn more about you in your résumé. Keep it short, authentic, and focused with enthusiasm.

Your Résumé

Your résumé summarizes your education, skills, experience, and other personal information that would qualify you for the job you are seeking. It must be easy to read because the scan time might initially be only 10 to 15 seconds. If you pass that initial eye scan, chances are very good that someone will read your entire résumé more carefully and with interest. That means your visual presentation must be orderly, engaging, attractive, not overwhelming, and *brief*. Limit it to one page if possible. Some industries might expect more comprehensive and detailed information. Research your intended audience to learn what they usually expect.

Experts agree that there is no single correct method or style. Research your employment setting and specific job requirements to sufficiently address both the *minimum* qualifications (MQs) and the *desirable* qualifications (DQs) specified. Address these with clarity so there is no confusion in the mind of the reader. Treat your résumé as your personal passkey or virtual marketing representative. Write clearly to articulate your key credentials and create a dynamic profile of who you are and the value you will bring to an employment setting.

Create a document that advertises your credentials and worth to a company. A résumé is not a short story—but it *is* a summary of *your* unique story about who you are and what you have to offer. Your story should convey your theme, and you should make certain that your theme is relevant to the position and employment setting to which you are applying. Only you can decide what your theme should be. If you have a particular history of successfully networking with clients and mentoring them, clearly express that theme. If you have a history of excellent leadership experiences, even including volunteer positions, share that with confidence. Perhaps you have some technical knowledge or specialized skills that you believe help you stand above other candidates. Express this professionally and enthusiastically. Your résumé will either get the attention of the reader and serve as the passkey that opens the interview door—or it will blend in with all the hundreds of other résumés that are so boring to read that they often are tossed into the wastebasket.

The Job Interview

The job interview is your opportunity to share your story. First impressions can often be lasting impressions, so be warm and friendly as you meet your interviewer or committee of interviewers. Offer a firm handshake, and be willing to talk about whatever topic the lead interviewer brings up to break the ice. It might be a comment about the weather, a local or national news story, or simply a question about the ease with which you were able to negotiate the traffic or find a parking space. Be gracious and personable. The interview questions will come soon enough, but you now have a few moments to establish a rapport with your audience, and this might even involve a bit of humor. Take advantage of this moment to bond!

You will no doubt respond to questions individually or in a small group, perhaps even over several different meetings. Use each question to tell a little bit more about your story, and use each question to carefully elaborate on your themes—the main three or four ideas you want to convey about your uniqueness. Do this carefully. Make sure you answer the specific question, and then expand your response in a seamless way that is engaging, holds the interest of the listeners, and provides your audience with more important and useful information about yourself and your value to them. Don't overtalk. It is wiser to offer a brief response than to go on for an extended time. Don't provide long-winded answers and *do not fake an answer!* If you don't know the answer, tell them you don't know the answer. People appreciate authenticity and honesty.

Your sharing must provide your interviewers with a clear understanding about your qualifications and the uniqueness of your personality. They need to believe that you indeed *are* the best person who can do the job, add value to the company, and absolutely fit into their "family" or company culture.

Bring a small notebook to jot down questions that are asked. That way, you will be certain to respond appropriately to the specific questions and keep track of the names of the various people at the interview, especially if there are more than three or four. Maintain eye contact, scanning all the persons in the room, but making certain to focus back onto the person who initially asked you the question. Do sufficient research and be prepared to ask several of your own questions when invited to do so—especially including a question about the timetable for their decision-making process and next anticipated steps.

Always end with a brief and sincere thank-you to each member of the interviewing committee, and use this moment to once again share your enthusiasm about being considered for the position and your desire to work with their team. Provide a firm handshake with each of them, thanking them for their time.

Review your responses to "Occupational Research" on pages 72–74 in Part V and your responses in Appendix 1 to prepare your cover letter, résumé, and job interviews.

PERSONAL COACHING TOOLS FOR STRESS REDUCTION, TIME MANAGEMENT, AND SETTING GOALS

Energy TimePlot©

Use the Energy TimePlot to chart your energy levels during the day. Then use that information to manage your stress levels.

1. On the horizontal axis of the graph below, circle the times that you typically get up in the morning and go to sleep at night.

2. Plot across the day, marking an X at your HIGH ENERGY times (10 = high) when you feel very good, think quickly, and are creative and productive, and also at your LOW ENERGY times (1 = low) when you feel drained and tired, sluggish, and tend to make mistakes. (For instance, if you wake up at 7 a.m. and are ready to go, with very high energy, you would mark an X inside the graph at the intersection of 7 a.m. on the horizontal axis and 9 or 10 on the vertical axis.)

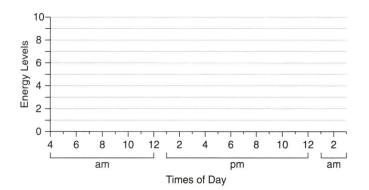

3. After completing steps 1 and 2 above, review your energy plot and place a T at any point where you experience TIME PRESSURE and an S at any point where you experience STRESS. Note the *causes* of your T's and S's by writing a short descriptive word next to them (such as "traffic," "homework," "biology class," "time with friends or family," etc.). Then reflect on ways to make appropriate changes to your daily routine to alleviate your stress.

The following activities will further assist you with discovering solutions and balancing your career and life roles.

The Scoop on Stress

Have you ever stayed awake at night worrying about something or someone? Have you ever been under pressure to do something and were very concerned about the outcome? Have you ever worried about tests and schoolwork, or perhaps a difficult relationship you experienced or saw others experiencing? Is your schedule so busy that sometimes you feel everything and everybody around you seems to suck the energy right out of you and there's no place to go for a quiet rest?

You're not alone. Everyone experiences stress at times—adults, teens, and even children. There are things you can do to minimize your stress and manage the stress that's unavoidable. Let's understand the scoop on stress.

What Is Stress?

Stress is a feeling that occurs when we react to certain situations or have interactions with others, including thoughts and perceptions we have even when we are alone. It's the body's way of responding to something that is out of the ordinary. It could be something challenging like giving a speech or making a class presentation or breaking up with someone with whom we shared a close relationship.

Some stressful situations can be positive. We respond to those difficult situations with increased focus, strength, and a resolve to meet the challenges head-on and prevail. We might know we feel stressed, but we are not incapacitated by our stress. We use it to be strong and do what needs to be done. Other stressful situations seem overwhelming, and we might experience panic and fear based on some strong sense of a *real* danger to ourselves or others, or a *perceived* danger or threatening situation.

From a purely physiological standpoint, stress is a set of responses or automatic reactions caused by "stressors." *Stressors* are a wide range of unpleasant sensory or psychological experiences—whatever it is we are trying to avoid (a person, place, thing, or situation). *Acute stressors* or *stress events* cause a set of stress reactions we normally recognize as our heart pounding, our mouth getting very dry, and perhaps a sudden flood of "butterflies" in our stomach. This is called the *stress response*.

Humans are well equipped to deal with stress—*if* it doesn't happen too often. But if stress keeps occurring, over and over again, a person's health and life can be threatened.

Your Body's Response to Stress

The first stage of the vital stress response involves the *sympathetic-adreno-medullary axis* (SAM) and is known best as the "fight-or-flight" response. To illustrate, imagine you are a cave person taking a walk looking for food. You hear a large tree branch snap on the ground behind you. You turn and look. How would you feel if you suddenly see a large hungry saber-tooth tiger approaching?

This is what happens to your body physiologically: Your brain perceives danger and sends the "danger/alert" message down your spinal cord to the adrenal medulla, or core of your adrenal glands. The adrenal glands pump adrenaline to prepare for the physical exertion that you will face—whether you choose to fight the tiger or run for cover. Your heart joins right in and starts pumping, which raises your blood pressure to quickly send blood to the parts of your body you will be using to either fight the good fight or quickly run away. Your liver steps in too, and starts pouring out glucose and calling up all your fat reserves to be immediately processed into triglycerides for super energy. Your circulatory system diverts your blood flow from your nonessential body functions—such as digestion and sexual functioning—to your arms, legs, and eyes to help you in the fight or flight.

After 5 to 10 minutes, your body automatically makes all the necessary changes to stabilize and replenish itself because your body somehow seems to know that you either won the fight or ran away safely to cover. This second phase involves the *hypothalamic-pituitary-adrenocortical axis* (HPA). If you ran into a saber-tooth tiger, your body really needs the HPA response to kick in after your fight or flight so your physiology can stabilize.

However, these days we normally don't run into large, hungry saber-tooth tigers. We do find ourselves experiencing stress from many different situations—such as oversleeping and being late for class, being caught in traffic jams, being unprepared for a big test, feeling overwhelmed from trying to accomplish too many tasks, being in debt, or having difficulties in our personal relationships, to name just a few examples. Also, we often experience perceived threats are just that—*perceived* and not real.

Our bodies do not know the difference between a saber-tooth tiger and a traffic jam and automatically respond to many stressful situations with the fight or flight syndrome, thus triggering both SAM *and* HPA!

Over time with *chronic stress,* this activation of the stress response results in elevated blood pressure that takes a toll on the arteries and circulatory system. The extra fats and glucose that are released during the stress response don't get metabolized right away, so they stay in the bloodstream and contribute to a buildup of plaque that forms within the walls of the blood vessels and can lead to heart disease and strokes. Chronic stress can lower your immune system. Stress also can bring on angina (chest pain), arrhythmia (irregular heart rhythms), and even a heart attack or stroke. Stress can worsen conditions such as type 2 diabetes, asthma, or gastrointestinal problems, and can even lead to depression.

Coping with Stress

Remember, the overall goal is to deal with stress actively and effectively. Research indicates that *anyone* can learn to cope better. That's called stress management, and that's great news! The key to reducing stress is to prevent it. Getting enough sleep, having a proper diet, avoiding excess caffeine and other stimulants, and taking time out to relax are helpful.

It's important to note the difference between good stress and bad stress. The stress response is very useful during emergency situations, such as when a parent rushes over to catch a toddler from falling off a playground jungle gym, or when a driver has to slam on the brakes to avoid hitting a child running onto the street. It can also be activated in a milder form at times when there is some pressure but no immediate danger— like being the field goal kicker in the last seconds of a tied Super Bowl game, or sitting down for a final exam, assuming you studied for it! This stress can be very useful and help keep you focused and ready to rise to the challenge.

Ongoing events—like coping with a divorce, moving to a new neighborhood or school, being in a difficult job or relationship, or dealing with the illness of a loved one—can also cause stress. Long-term stressful situations can produce a lasting, low-level stress that can be very challenging both emotionally and physically. The nervous system senses continued pressure and may remain slightly activated and continue to pump out extra stress hormones over an extended period. This can wear out the body's reserves, leave a person feeling depleted or overwhelmed, weaken the body's immune system, and cause other problems.

You can find more information about stress—including the effects of stress, stress reduction, stress in the workplace, and emotional support—at the Web site of the American Institute of Stress (www.stress.org).

Stressors & Solutions©

Review "Evaluating My Present Career-Life Roles" in Appendix 1 to prepare for this activity.

Below are examples of common stressors that affect many college students and people experiencing career and life transitions. Read through the list and then complete steps 1 through 3.

1. On the blank lines at the bottom of the list, add several items that are personal stressors for you.

2. To the left of each item, check all those that give you the greatest difficulty. Indicate whether they are *imposed stressors* (I) or *self-inflicted* stressors (S) by circling I or S.

3. Reflect on all those you checked, and in the right-hand column list practical solutions that will help you make progress toward reducing stress. Create solutions you *will* do.

	Stresses	Solutions
☐	Pressure from others (I or S)	_____
☐	Money/debt concerns (I or S)	_____
☐	Too many classes (I or S)	_____
☐	Indecision (I or S)	_____
☐	Too much homework (I or S)	_____
☐	Too little sleep (I or S)	_____
☐	Lack of self-discipline (I or S)	_____
☐	Too much socializing (I or S)	_____
☐	Poor attitude (I or S)	_____
☐	Family demands (I or S)	_____
☐	Low self-esteem (I or S)	_____
☐	Procrastination (I or S)	_____
☐	Unclear personal goals (I or S)	_____
☐	Unclear career goals (I or S)	_____
☐	Personal disorganization (I or S)	_____
☐	Perfectionism (I or S)	_____
☐	Poor time management (I or S)	_____
☐	Attempting too much (I or S)	_____
☐	Relationship difficulties (I or S)	_____
☐	Difficulty setting priorities (I or S)	_____
☐	_____ (I or S)	_____
☐	_____ (I or S)	_____
☐	_____ (I or S)	_____

Stress Busters©

Develop a list of positive responses to stress and practice using them. Make copies of your list, putting one in your wallet or purse, one on your desk, one on your refrigerator at home, and one on your bedroom mirror or anywhere it will be easily accessible for you to review when stressful times arise. The following are some suggestions for your list.

- *Breathing:* Stop, close your eyes, turn your attention inward, and *breathe*. Breathe in through your nose and out through your lips. Focus your attention on your breath, noticing how it flows in and out easily. When you notice yourself "thinking" about something else, allow yourself to return to noticing your breath. You can do this using 4 or 5 deep breaths or more—anytime, anywhere. It works!

- *Shifting perception:* Learn to look at people, situations, and events that cause you stress through a different lens, sometimes even through the eyes of another with whom you are having difficulty. Turn obstacles into opportunities and stumbling blocks into stepping-stones. Be willing to shift from your normal paradigms to new paradigms that can stretch you toward personal growth.

- *Meditation:* There are many types of meditation. The breathing exercise above can be used as a way to quiet the mind for 20 minutes, once or twice a day (mornings and evenings). The practice teaches your mind to "let go" of thoughts and feelings and return to a "center"—a place of peace. Research shows that the physiological benefits of meditation can reduce the risk of heart disease by lowering blood pressure.

- *Exercise:* Regular exercise is helpful in releasing stress and maintaining health. Examples include dancing, walking, working out, jogging, self-massage, and swimming.

- Do something that's fun and spontaneous!

- Call a friend. Ask her or him to remind you of who you are—that you are a terrific person—because you might have forgotten!

- Pray or take time to reflect. Get in touch with whatever might be inside or outside of yourself that you feel some connection with, that you feel is greater than you and that brings you comfort and peace. Spend some time reflecting on this and listen.

- Maintain proper nutrition.

- Relax in a hot bath—especially with sea salts.

- Read one of your favorite books or magazines.

- Try journal writing.

- Take up a hobby

- Place a favorite picture—your family, your pet, or perhaps a peaceful ocean scene—close to your work space.

- Join or start a support group.

- Be willing to honestly express your needs to others.

- Be less critical of yourself.

- Note any unreasonable expectations you might have.

- Learn how to have passion without attachment.

- List any of your own ideas that will work for you:

_____

_____

_____

Time Tools©: A Time Management Worksheet

The following tools are useful for setting priorities. They are logical and will help you break through any barriers of feeing stuck and off track. They are easy to understand and easy to implement. The "1, 2, 3" Rule deals with prioritizing activities. Once you do this activity, continue on to the 80/20 Rule.

The "1, 2, 3" Rule

A. List all the activities you have on your "Daily Plate" in the first column of the table below.

B. In the space provided next to it in the first column, identify each activity with a number 1 through 3—with 1 = *Must Do* because of deadlines or outside influences, 2 = *Should Do* because it is important but does *not* have deadlines or outside influences, and 3 = *Like to Do* because it would be wonderful to accomplish this activity, but in actuality there is no impending deadline or outside influence, and it really is not as important as priorities 1 or 2.

C. Rewrite the *top five* items that you rated as "1" into the middle column ("1 = Must Do"). Then prioritize them as accurately as possible in the blank spaces next to each item—using 1 to indicate the most important and 5 for the least important.

D. Transfer these top five items to the final list on the far right ("1 = Must Do Prioritized").

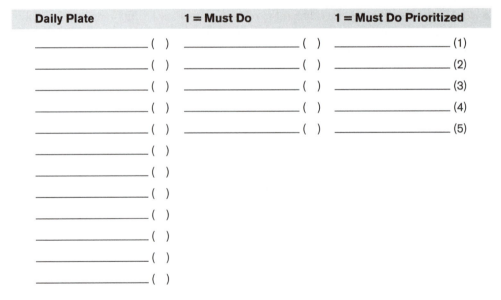

Daily Plate	1 = Must Do	1 = Must Do Prioritized
_____ ( )	_____ ( )	_____ (1)
_____ ( )	_____ ( )	_____ (2)
_____ ( )	_____ ( )	_____ (3)
_____ ( )	_____ ( )	_____ (4)
_____ ( )	_____ ( )	_____ (5)
_____ ( )		
_____ ( )		
_____ ( )		
_____ ( )		
_____ ( )		
_____ ( )		
_____ ( )		

Now go to the next activity, "The 80/20 Rule."

The 80/20 Rule

The 80/20 Rule, also called *Pareto's Principle,* was suggested in the late 1940s by management thinker Joseph M. Juran. He named it after the Italian economist Vilfredo Pareto, who had observed that 80% of the wealth went to 20% of the population. The theory has since been applied to other areas of modern life—the basic assumption being that most results in any situation are determined by a small number of causes. This idea is often applied to data such as sales figures: "20% of clients are responsible for 80% of sales volume." Such a statement is testable, is likely to be approximately correct, and might be helpful in decision making. (You can Google "80/20 rule" to learn more information about this concept.)

To apply the 80/20 Rule to your own situation, first review your list of five activities under "1 = Must Do Prioritized" in the last column of the table above. Because 20% of 5 is 1, if you do the #1-prioritized activity on your daily plate, you will have accomplished 80% of what you truly need to be doing that day. Now you can go to the items ranked as 2 or 3, or just do something else. Buy an ice cream cone if you like! Go to a museum! You will still have accomplished 80% of what had to be done using the 80/20 Rule.

Review and re-rank your list as needed and apply the 80/20 Rule to move through your Daily Plate of activities. You might want to modify this chart and create a Weekly Plate or Monthly Plate.

Pie-Charting©: A Time Management Worksheet

Step 1: How You Are Currently Using Your Time

In the first column of the table below, list five usual tasks that you presently do from day-to-day (or week-to-week). Then reflect on the percentage of the day or week you spend on these tasks, and enter your estimate in the second column (homework = 20%, socializing = 25%, etc.). Then in the third column, rank these tasks according to the amount of time they consume. For instance, the task that takes up the largest percentage of your time would receive Priority Rank 1, and so forth until you rank all five tasks. Now in the last column, make a pie chart to reflect these percentages and rankings. This shows how you presently use your time.

Tasks I *Am Doing* Now	% of Day/Week	Priority Rank #	Time/Task Pie
_____	_____	_____	
_____	_____	_____	
_____	_____	_____	
_____	_____	_____	
_____	_____	_____	

Step 2: How You *Should* Use Your Time

In the first column of the table below, list five tasks that you *need to do* daily or weekly. Then in the second column, identify the task that *should have* top priority and rank it #1. Rank the task with second priority as 2, and so forth for all five tasks. In the third column, indicate the estimated percentage of the day or week you need to spend on these tasks, based on your priority rankings. Now in the last column, make a pie chart to reflect these rankings and percentages. This shows how you can better manage your time to be successful in college!

Tasks I *Need to Do* Now	Priority Rank #	% of Day/Week	Time/Task Pie
_____	_____	_____	
_____	_____	_____	
_____	_____	_____	
_____	_____	_____	
_____	_____	_____	